STANDING FOR
LIGHT AND TRUTH

STANDING
FOR
LIGHT
AND
TRUTH

ADRIAN ROGERS

CROSSWAY BOOKS

A DIVISION OF
GOOD NEWS PUBLISHERS
WHEATON, ILLINOIS

Standing for Light and Truth

Copyright © 2003 by Adrian Rogers

Published by Crossway Books
                A division of Good News Publishers
                1300 Crescent Street
                Wheaton, Illinois 60187

Cover design & photo: Bellevue Baptist Church &
                            Love Worth Finding Ministries

First printing, 2003

Printed in the United States of America

Unless otherwise indicated, Bible quotations are taken from the King James Version.

Library of Congress Cataloging-in-Publication Data
Rogers, Adrian.
    Standing for light and truth / Adrian Rogers.
       p. cm.
    ISBN 1-58134-556-9 (hc : alk. paper)
    1. Christian life—Meditations. 2. Christian life—Biblical teaching. I Title.
BV4501.3.R655   2003
248.4'861—dc22
                                                2003019240

LB		13	12	11	10	09	08	07	06	05	04	03
15	14	13	12	11	10	9	8	7	6	5	4	3	2	1

This book is warmly and gratefully dedicated to the following men who have served as deacon chairmen since I have been pastor of Bellevue Baptist Church. To be the chairman of deacons at Bellevue Baptist Church is a great honor and a tremendous responsibility. The deacons at Bellevue Baptist Church have incredible fellowship. They do not see themselves as managers of the church, nor men appointed to oversee the pastor. They present themselves with a Christlike spirit to serve the church.

Bellevue Baptist Church is operated under this philosophy: The church is pastor-led, deacon-served, committee-operated, and congregationally approved. That works wonderfully well for us.

The following men are some of my dearest friends, and I thank God for them. Some are already in heaven but are still held in my heart. Would to God every pastor could have deacons like these:

JEFF L. ARNOLD   BRYAN MILLER   CHUCK TAYLOR

HARRY SMITH   STEVE TUCKER   GENE HOWARD

DR. ROBERT VINCENT   DAVID PERDUE   JIM GLOVER

CHARLES BRAND   ROLAND MADDOX   JIM ANGEL

BOB DAWKINS   ROBERT FARGARSON   JOHN CROCKETT

R. L. SORRELL   AL CHILDRESS   PAUL STOVALL

DR. DEWEY BURTON—DECEASED

WILLIAM B. MILLS—DECEASED

Contents

Acknowledgments

I want to thank the people whose support, encouragement, and faithful work helped make this book possible: the staff at Love Worth Finding Ministries; Linda Glance, my faithful secretary; President Lane Dennis, Vice President Marvin Padgett, Managing Editor Ted Griffin, and all the helpful people at Crossway Books; and my editor and friend, Philip Rawley. You are all the greatest and dear friends.

Also, I wish to acknowledge the membership of the dear church that received these messages with open hearts and minds. What an encouragement they continue to be to me.

Introduction

O send out thy light and thy truth: let them lead me;
let them bring me unto thy holy hill, and to thy
tabernacles.

PSALM 43:3

This Scripture is written boldly across the large cornice over the entrance of Bellevue Baptist Church. It represents the heartbeat of the church. This congregation that numbers over 28,000 members is celebrating 100 years of glorious history. The church, though a century old, is alive, vigorous, and growing greatly.

I have personally had the joy of pastoring Bellevue for thirty-one years. No pastor has ever had a more loving congregation and greater joy in his task. What is the secret of the dynamism of this exciting congregation?

For all of its history Bellevue has never argued or quibbled about the great doctrines of the Christian faith. For the people of Bellevue, light and truth include such convictions as:

1. The inerrant and infallible Word of God.
2. The deity of the virgin-born Son of God.
3. The saving and transforming power of the gospel.
4. The irrevocable commitment to the Great Commission.
5. The call to holy living.

These and other cherished beliefs have helped bind together this great fellowship.

The people at Crossway Books were kind enough to ask that some of the messages I have delivered at Bellevue be put into this volume. Light and truth was selected as the theme.

The reader will recognize these messages as sermons, for that is what they are. They are not literary masterpieces, but the pulpit pleadings and the passionate heart of a pastor. They were used of God when first delivered in the worship center at Bellevue. My prayer is that they will be used of God again in your heart as you read them.

I have endeavored to give the sources of quotations and ideas where known, but these are messages prepared in the course of a pastor's week and are not scholarly dissertations. These are thoughts gathered from my notebook and ideas picked up by years of reading. I apologize if I have not always given proper credit. The preacher milks many cows to churn his own butter.

May God send forth His light and His truth into your life.

Adrian Rogers
Senior Pastor
Bellevue Baptist Church
Memphis, Tennessee

PART I

STANDING
FOR
LIGHT

1

Christ the Light

*Jesus—Heaven's Light for
Earth's Darkness*

I heard of an English professor who walked into his classroom one day and wrote these words on the blackboard: "Walk with light." He then asked the students who wrote these words.

The students, supposing the phrase to be a profound thought from a great work of literature, guessed various authors. Some said Goethe, others Emerson, and still others guessed the poet Wordsworth. But the professor said, "No, I read these words on the traffic light on my way to the school this morning."

"Walk with light" is a profound thought, even when it is delivered in the most ordinary circumstances. Indeed, this is what God did when He sent His precious Son, the Lord Jesus Christ, to earth to walk among men. Jesus Himself said He came as "the light of the world" (John 8:12) to save ordinary people like you and me. The apostle John declared that we should make it our ambition as Christians to "walk in the light, as he [Jesus] is in the light" (1 John 1:7).

I want us to see the profound nature of light as it is used to reveal God in all of His holiness and purity in Scripture. Light itself is so mysterious. The great physicist Albert Einstein is reported to have said, "For the rest of my life I want to reflect on what light is."

The nature of light is nearly impossible to define. Is it a wave without a medium, or a particle without a mass? Look up the word *light* in the dictionary, and you will see that even brilliant minds struggle for words and concepts to define light. Perhaps this is why the Holy Spirit chose light as a metaphor for God throughout the Scripture. Like God, light is mysterious but glorious. Let's learn some lessons about God's light from the apostle John, so that we won't be in the dark about light.

THE UNCHANGING CONSTANCY OF GOD'S LIGHT

The opening verses of John 1 are the New Testament equivalent of the opening verses of Genesis 1, and that is not by coincidence. The apostle wants us to understand that Jesus is the eternal God, who was present at the creation of the world. John wrote: "In the beginning was the Word, and the Word was with God, and the Word was God. The same was in the beginning with God" (vv. 1-2).

This is one of the greatest statements of Jesus' eternal, unchanging nature as the Second Person of the Godhead in all of the New Testament. It is very interesting that both John (vv. 4-9) and Jesus Himself refer to Jesus as the light, because light by its nature, like our Lord, is constant. The speed and the nature of light never change.

The world has marveled at Einstein's theory of relativity, which Einstein said he was able to construct because the speed of light is the one thing in the world of nature that is unchangeable. It is the only constant in this physical universe in which we live.

Einstein came up with the famous formula $E = MC^2$. This

means that the energy of any given object equals its mass times the speed of light squared. I am told that only twelve other men besides Einstein truly understand this. I can't vouch for that because I do not know who the other eleven may be!

Seriously, the truth is that if you can explain Einstein's formula, I need to talk to you. But I do know that light travels at the speed of 186,282 miles per second. That speed is many times around the world in one tick of the clock, which is really beyond our ability to conceive.

We can understand the basic concept of relative speed. If I pass you at fifty miles per hour, that can be measured. A police officer with a radar gun can clock my speed. Now if we pass each other from opposite directions at fifty miles per hour, the relative speed is one hundred miles per hour. And if I am traveling at fifty miles per hour and you travel alongside me at fifty-six miles per hour, then your speed relative to mine is six miles per hour faster.

But suppose you highjack a light beam and travel at 186,282 miles per second, and I am riding another light beam headed in the opposite direction. We will pass each other, but our relative speed will not double. The rules have changed because the speed of light is constant.

It is not speed that is now altered, but time. When the speed of light is reached, time basically stands still. The nearer we come to the speed of light, the more time slows down. In other words, we must adjust our normal understanding to conform to the nature of light, because light is not going to change or vary its constancy to accommodate our limited minds.

So it is with our God. Albert Einstein demonstrated that the speed of light is unchanging, but the apostle John saw the unchangeable nature of God's light before Einstein ever saw the light of day. John understood that there is no variableness with God's light. The Lord Jesus is the everlasting, unchanging light of all eternity.

The apostle James, the half-brother of Jesus, also testified to the perfect constancy of God's light: "Every good gift and every perfect gift is from above, and cometh down from the Father of lights, with whom is no variableness, neither shadow of turning" (James 1:17).

As is the Father, so is the Son. There is no shadow of turning with Jesus. It is always high noon with Him. His love never has a sunset so as to need a sunrise. He never stops shining, and He cannot change. We can bask in the light of His love even when everything around us is dark.

Our need and desire for light is so ingrained in us that someone devised the ingenious system known as daylight saving time to give us more daylight during the summer. I read that the idea for daylight saving time came from an old Indian who cut off one end of his blanket and sewed it to the other end to make the blanket longer. We think we are changing time and altering the sunlight by setting our clocks ahead or back one hour for a brief period of time. But all we are doing is changing our perception of time in relation to the sunlight.

Praise God for the unchanging constancy of His light. When at last in heaven we are made like Him, we will have His nature, which is perfect light. But we must first undergo the transformation of the Rapture to stand in God's presence, for the Bible says that God is "the blessed and only Potentate, the King of kings, and Lord of lords; who only hath immortality, dwelling in the light which no man can approach unto; whom no man hath seen, nor can see: to whom be honour and power everlasting" (1 Timothy 6:15-16).

What a glory that will be when Jesus returns for us and takes us to be with Him forever. Time will stand still, and we will dwell in the perfect light of heaven. The glories of heaven make the horrors of hell even more unbearable. Jesus described hell as "outer darkness," the total absence of light. And while in heaven time will stand still, in hell time will never end.

This same apostle John said of those who are judged and sent to hell for worshiping the Antichrist in the Tribulation: "The smoke of their torment ascendeth up for ever and ever: and they have no rest day nor night, who worship the beast and his image, and whosoever receiveth the mark of his name" (Revelation 14:11). Thank God for the Lord Jesus, the everlasting, unchanging Light of eternity who has delivered us from the power of darkness and transferred us into His glorious kingdom (Colossians 1:13).

Do you realize that our faith rests on the unchanging constancy of Jesus Christ? I once had an opportunity to witness for two hours to Muhammad Ali, the former heavyweight boxing champion. Ali, who is a Muslim, asked me this question: "If you say that Jesus is the Son of God because He was born of a virgin, wouldn't that make Adam more the son of God than Jesus because Adam did not have either a father or a mother?"

I said to him, "Champ, Jesus is not the Son of God because He was born of a virgin. He was born of a virgin because He is the Son of God." Jesus never had a beginning. He is the Eternal Son, the unchanging One, "the same yesterday, and to day, and for ever" (Hebrews 13:8).

Not only does our eternal destiny depend on Jesus Christ's unchanging nature, but so does the very survival of this universe. If Jesus Christ were ever to change or for one second cease being who He is, this world would literally fly apart. "He is before all things, and by him all things consist" (Colossians 1:17). The word "consist" means "hold together." Jesus is the "glue" that holds creation together.

Isn't it wonderful to know that God never changes? A wise man once said, "You can't make God nervous." What can disturb Him? The hymn-writer expressed it so well: "Great is Thy faithfulness, O God my Father; there is no shadow of turning with Thee; Thou changest not, Thy compassions they fail not; As Thou hast been Thou forever wilt be."

THE UNFAILING VITALITY OF THIS LIGHT

In John 1 we find another characteristic of the light that is Jesus Christ. This light has life-giving power. "All things were made by him; and without him was not any thing made that was made. In him was life; and the life was the light of men" (vv. 3-4).

There can be no life in the physical world without light. One of the first big words I learned in school was *photosynthesis*, which literally means put together with light. It is amazing to grasp the degree to which life on this planet depends on photosynthesis, the process by which green plants and other organisms use light to convert various elements into glucose. For instance, glucose is a simple sugar that is the basic energy source for virtually all organisms on earth. In addition, the oxygen we need to breathe and stay alive is produced as a by-product of photosynthesis. Even the so-called fossil fuels such as coal and petroleum that we have come to depend on so heavily are by-products of photosynthesis, which in turn needs the light of the sun to occur.

If the sun were to cease to shine, all physical life on this planet would soon cease to exist. The first recorded words that God spoke in the Bible were, "Let there be light" (Genesis 1:3). When

God began to turn a chaos into a cosmos, He brought forth light. God doesn't have to take your life for you to cease to exist. All He has to do is stop giving it. If God were to withhold the light, photosynthesis would be impossible, and we would suffocate without oxygen.

Spiritually, the same is true. There is no life without the light of Jesus. But when He shines on our lives, a spiritual photosynthesis takes place, and new life is produced. There is vitality in the Lord Jesus Christ.

My own life is a testimony to this glorious reality. I was in darkness and confusion as a teenage boy. I wanted to know for certain that my sins were forgiven and that I was a child of God; so I decided to get it settled. I will never forget the day I stopped at the corner of Calvin Avenue and 39th Street in West Palm Beach, Florida, looked straight up into the heavens, and prayed something like this: "O God, I don't know whether I am lost and the Holy Spirit has me under conviction, or whether I am saved and the devil is trying to make me doubt it. But one thing I know now for certain is that You died for my sins and that salvation is totally by grace. By an act of my faith, I receive You as my Lord and Savior. Come into my heart, forgive my sin, and save me. I don't look for a sign, and I don't ask for a feeling. I just stand on Your Word."

When I did that, God's light flooded my heart, and a spiritual photosynthesis took place. Jesus, who turned a chaos into a cosmos in the first creation, turned the chaos of my life into something wonderful when He made me a new creation. I began to experience the reality of Jesus' promise, "I am the light of the world: he that followeth me shall not walk in darkness, but shall have the light of life" (John 8:12).

THE UNCORRUPTED PURITY OF THIS LIGHT

Allow me to point you to a third quality of God's light, which is its uncompromising purity that nothing can stain or corrupt. I direct you to verse 5 of John 1, where John continued his description of the Lord Jesus with these words: "And the light shineth in darkness; and the darkness comprehended it not."

Nothing known to man is as pure as sunlight in the natural world, and nothing in this universe is as pure as the spiritual light of the Lord Jesus. John makes this clear in his first epistle: "This then is the message which we have heard of him, and declare unto you, that God is light, and in him is no darkness at all" (1 John 1:5).

We need to put John 1:5 and 1 John 1:5 together as two strong pillars in support of the truth that Jesus is uncompromised, unadulterated purity.

Light is a wonderful symbol of our Lord because light cannot be defiled by any medium that it passes through or any substance that it falls upon. This is true of nothing else in the natural world. Pure water from a spring is soon defiled by whatever it touches. Crystal-white snow falls upon the earth and becomes filthy and dingy.

Light, however, cannot be contaminated by anything it falls upon or passes through. This is true of light in any form, whether natural or artificial, and it is abundantly true of God's holy light. This speaks to us of the unsullied holiness of God and the stainless purity of the Lord Jesus Christ. He is light that cannot be defiled and cannot defile.

What a picture of the Savior! Jesus touched sinners wherever He went here on earth, but sin never touched Him. Jesus could look upon a woman brought to Him from the very act of adultery (John 8:1-11), expose and forgive her sin, and yet not be defiled by what He saw.

Jesus' purity shone brightly during His temptation by the devil in the wilderness (Matthew 4:1-11). Jesus was tempted, not to show that He could sin, but to prove that He could not. It is impossible for the sinless Light of the world to be contaminated in any way. We have a Savior "who is holy, harmless, undefiled, separate from sinners, and made higher than the heavens" (Hebrews 7:26).

God's pure light shines in the darkness and lays bare all evil. The moment light appears, darkness is vanquished. Darkness is the absence of light; so by definition darkness is no more when light comes.

What an example Jesus' purity ought to be to those of us who are children of the light. We need to understand that we have no real fellowship with this dark world. The apostle Paul wrote: "Be ye not unequally yoked together with unbelievers: for what fellowship hath righteousness with unrighteousness? and what communion hath light with darkness?" (2 Corinthians 6:14).

Jesus said, "Ye are the light of the world. A city that is set on an hill cannot be hid" (Matthew 5:14). We are to shine as lights in a dark world. But we are to be pure as Jesus is pure. We hear much today about the separation of church and state. Perhaps we need to have more preaching and teaching on the separation of church and world. We must not let the light that is within us become darkness by allowing ourselves to become defiled by this world.

THE UNCONQUERED MAJESTY OF THIS LIGHT

There is another glorious truth about the Lord Jesus in John 1:5, which we find in the second half of this wonderful verse: "And the light shineth in darkness; and the darkness comprehended it not."

Other Bible translations render the phrase "the darkness comprehended it not" in various ways: "the darkness has not overcome it," "has not put it out," or "can never extinguish it." Whatever the exact words, the message is the same. Jesus Christ stands as the unconquered Ruler of time and eternity.

All of history is a battle between light and darkness. God's kingdom is a kingdom of light, and Satan's kingdom is a kingdom of darkness. The devil is the prince of darkness—"Lucifer, son of the morning" (Isaiah 14:12)—who sinned against God and became Satan, the father of the night.

Satan is a formidable foe, but the grand truth is that darkness is totally powerless against the light. Don't get the idea that there is a raging battle between God and Satan, and we are waiting breathlessly to see its outcome. Don't ever think that the kingdom of darkness is somehow as strong as the kingdom of light.

Have you ever played the game of antonyms, in which you supply the opposite of a word that is given to you? In this game if I say up, you say down. If I say good, you say bad. If I say rich, you say poor.

Now if I were to say God, many people would automatically answer Satan. But that would not be correct, for Satan is not the opposite of God. God has no opposite that is equal to Him in power or authority. Satan's darkness is not the opposite of God's light, but the absence of it.

Therefore, Satan and his kingdom of darkness must bow before God and the majesty of His light. It is a fact in the natural world that when light comes, darkness must go. There is not enough darkness in the entire universe to put out the light of one candle.

This means there is only one way to get rid of darkness when it is present. The horrible events of September 11 and its aftermath in the war on terror and the recent war in Iraq have demonstrated that when we encounter darkness, we cannot curse it out, shoot it out, or bomb it out. We may temporarily put some practitioners of darkness out of business, but the only way to remove darkness is to release light.

We have learned that terrorism is the result of false religion, and all false religion is based in darkness. The only answer is the light of God's Word. We cannot ultimately overcome false religion by warfare. The only thing that will kill a lie is not a bomb or a bullet, but the truth.

There is no question about the ultimate outcome of the struggle between light and darkness because light has unconquerable power. The greatest source of light that we know of in our world is the sun. To look too long at the noonday sun is to put one's eyes out. The sun radiates more energy in one second than man has used since the beginning of civilization. Four million tons of hydrogen are destroyed every second in a nuclear explosion on the sun. And yet, for all of its tremendous power, the sun ripens a little bunch of grapes like it had nothing else to do.

This is an illustration of heaven's greater and brighter light. Our mighty Savior, who governs this universe, is concerned about the smallest matter of our lives. Not only does God love us all, but God loves us individually.

My wife, Joyce, and I love to walk on the beach. At sunset when the sun is setting over the ocean, there is a golden pathway that comes to us as we walk along. It is like God has put a path of liquid gold on the bosom of the sea. The unusual thing about this golden pathway is that it is coming directly to us. There may be another couple a hundred yards ahead of us, and that same golden pathway is also coming directly to them.

How much like God's love that is. We, each one of us, have God to ourselves, and yet He belongs to everyone. And we have victory in Jesus because no force on the earth or below the earth can stand against the mighty majesty of His light.

THE UNDIMMED GLORY OF THIS LIGHT

There is glory in God's light as well as majesty. If Jesus had not come to earth, the glory of God would have remained a concept forever locked in heaven. But the apostle John, one of the three who beheld Christ's glory on the Mount of Transfiguration (Matthew 17:1-9), left us this testimony: "And the Word was made flesh, and dwelt among us, (and we beheld his glory, the glory as of the only begotten of the Father,) full of grace and truth" (John 1:14).

John saw the glory of God in the face of Jesus Christ, and he, Peter, and James were dazzled by the sight. Just as artificial illumination can never match the flawless light of the sun, so no source of light in creation can begin to approach the undimmed glory of Jesus.

There are seven colors that comprise the spectrum of light that comes from the sun. But when all seven colors are combined, the result is pure white. The number seven speaks of the perfection of our Savior, for seven is the perfect number. And the totality of these in their whiteness speaks of His purity.

Without light there can be no sight and no color. The color we see is in the light. Take away the light, and you rob the world of color. The most glorious bouquet of flowers will dim and turn dark without light. Without Jesus the world and our lives would lose all color and grow exceedingly dark.

But thank God for the multicolored glory of God's marvelous

grace and light as revealed in Jesus. His light will never grow dim or fade, and He calls us to come to this light. We need not live in the darkness of our depravity outside of Christ, or in the cave of our carnality as disobedient Christians, for Jesus wants to light up our world with His eternal glory.

Your life will reflect all the glorious colors in the spectrum of His light when you give yourself completely and without reservation to Christ. The poet's experience will be yours: "Heaven above is softer blue, Earth around is sweeter green. Something lives in every hue Christless eyes have never seen; birds with gladder songs o'erflow, flowers with deeper beauty shine; since I know, as now I know, I am His, and He is mine."

THE UNCLAIMED VICTORY OF THIS LIGHT

When we see the awesome wonder and beauty of God's light as revealed in Jesus, we must shake our heads at the tragedy that some people have neglected or refused such light. The sad fact is that while no one can put out the light, they can shut it out by their sin and blindness. The victory over sin and hell that Jesus offers is free and eternal, but it must be claimed.

But sadly, the majority of the people to whom Jesus ministered rejected Him, as we read further in John 1: "That was the true Light, which lighteth every man that cometh into the world. He was in the world, and the world was made by him, and the world knew him not. He came unto his own, and his own received him not" (vv. 9-11).

This rejection was not only a reality in Jesus' day, but it is happening today. There are none so blind as those who refuse to see. Worse than a child afraid of the dark is a man afraid of the light. There is no greater sin than to reject light, because to reject the light is to refuse to believe in Jesus. This is greater than any moral sin. Jesus Himself spoke of the tragedy of unbelief:

> *He that believeth on him is not condemned: but he that believeth not is condemned already, because he hath not believed in the name of the only begotten Son of God. And this is the condemnation, that light is come into the world, and men loved darkness rather than light, because their deeds were evil. For every one that doeth evil hateth the light, neither cometh to the light, lest his deeds should be reproved. But he that doeth truth cometh to the light, that his deeds may be made manifest, that they are wrought in God.*
>
> —JOHN 3:18-21

God will judge men primarily not because of the sin they have committed, but because of the light that they have rejected. This is why we must send forth the Light of the World, who is Jesus, so that people may hear and believe the gospel.

And what a glorious promise we have to offer lost men and women as we contend for the truth: "But as many as received him, to them gave he power to become the sons of God, even to them that believe on his name" (John 1:12). Jesus is heaven's light for earth's darkness. Is He shining through your life to others?

2

Guided by Light

Detours, Dead Ends, and
Dry Holes

I was told recently about a humorous sign that was posted at a place of work: "Due to the heavy workload around here, the light at the end of the tunnel has been turned off until further notice."

Have you ever felt that someone had turned off the light at the end of your tunnel, that you were heading down a road with no illumination and no map? Some people may feel that way about their work, but the fact is that many of us have come to places in our lives where we seem to be traveling in the dark without any guidance. And so we wind up taking detours and back roads, and sometimes running into dead ends.

My friend, you may be in a place like this right now. And if you aren't now, you will be soon. Our lives seldom move from point to point in a nice straight line. But I have good news for you even if it seems the light has gone out at the end of your tunnel and you are crying out, "O God, where are You? I need Your guidance!"

The good news is that God does guide His people. The Bible says, "As many as are led by the Spirit of God, they are the sons of God" (Romans 8:14). God faithfully leads us, even when we find ourselves in unfamiliar and uncomfortable territory.

You may say, "Well, if God is leading me, something must be wrong. Either He doesn't know how to read a map, I don't know how to follow Him, or I am out of His will. If God is leading me, why do I keep getting off on detours and dead ends and end up at dry holes?"

I believe the insight concerning that is found in the Word of God. We are going to learn that God does lead us, that we're on the King's highway, and that it's a journey to joy with Jesus Christ as our companion, the Holy Spirit as our Guide, and the Bible as our map.

And yet we will also see that many times in this journey things do not turn out exactly the way we expect. There are a lot of unexpected detours and seeming dead ends on life's road, and it's not because God has turned off His guiding light or we have misread the map. He has some important lessons to teach us along the way. We can learn from the way God guided ancient Israel to the Promised Land.

THE DISCIPLINE OF DETOURS

The first discovery I want you to see concerning God's guiding light is the discipline of detours. In Exodus 13:17-18 we read what happened after the Pharaoh of Egypt had had enough of God's plagues as administered by Moses and told Moses to take the Israelites and leave Egypt:

> *And it came to pass, when Pharaoh had let the people go, that God led them not through the way of the land of the Philistines, although that was near; for God said, Lest peradventure the people repent when they see war, and they return to Egypt:*

But God led the people about, through the way of the wilderness of the Red sea: and the children of Israel went up harnessed out of the land of Egypt.

A Divine Detour with a Definite Purpose

Underscore the phrase "God led the people about." It means He led them in circles. The Bible tells us very clearly that God did not lead the people of Israel by a direct route but led them on a detour. And it wasn't a mistake. God did not lose His sense of direction. This was a divine detour with a definite purpose.

Why did God lead the Israelites this way? Why didn't He just lead them from Egypt to the land of Canaan by the shortest and most direct route? Well, a straight line may be the shortest distance between two points, but it's not always the best route. God has a purpose in His detours, and we are told His purpose in this instance.

God led His people on a detour because He knew that if they took a straight path it would lead them to the land of the war-like Philistines. Hundreds of years later, during the reign of King David, the Israelites would be more than a match for the Philistines. But not as a nation of newly freed slaves with multiplied thousands of women and little ones in their midst.

God knew that if the Israelites saw the Philistines, their hearts would melt with fear, and they would turn on their heels and go right back to Egypt—dismayed, discouraged, and defeated. So God didn't lead them that way because He knew they weren't ready for a battle.

Now make no mistake. There were plenty of battles ahead for Israel to fight. Their time for war would come, just as God has called us to a holy war "against principalities, against powers, against the rulers of the darkness of this world, against spiritual wickedness in high places" (Ephesians 6:12).

God knows what we are ready to face, and He will not throw us into the battle until we are ready. God has a land of blessing and fulfillment for you, even as He had for Israel. God has a job for you to do, and yet right now He may have you out in the wilderness going round and round in circles. And you may wonder if you are out of His will.

Now it may be that you are going around in circles because you haven't read the map right or listened to your guide. Only you can determine that as you seek the Lord. But I want to suggest that a detour may not be God's displeasure at all, but His discipline. God may be taking you the long way at this time because He knows you are not quite ready for some of the things He has in store for you. That winding road you're on may be the best indication that God is taking you somewhere special.

The Necessity of God's Boot Camp

God led the Israelites on a detour instead of taking them on the straightest route because sometimes it is possible to arrive too early. The army used to have a term for young, fuzzy-cheeked officers who were rushed through training and sent to the field. They were called "ninety-day wonders."

I've seen some ninety-day wonders in other fields. They go up like a rocket and come down like a rock. They are eager beavers who want it all, and want it all *now*. But I'm here to tell you that in God's plan, there are no fast and easy routes to the top. You cannot become a soldier in God's army without undergoing the discipline of boot camp.

This is why God led the Israelites "through the way of the

wilderness." Did you notice that description of their route in
Exodus 13:18? The wilderness was a place of hardness, thirst, and
rugged terrain. It was God's boot camp, a place of discipline where
He led the Israelites to toughen them up for the challenges ahead.
God was getting them ready for the conquest of the Promised
Land.

Now doubtless the people did not understand that at the time.
I am sure they wondered what was going on and why they were
heading into a desert. They didn't know all that God had in store
for them, but then they didn't have to know. It was enough that
God knew. Very likely, the Israelites had never even heard of the
Philistines. They didn't know what was out there ahead of them.
But God did, and He knew they weren't ready to go through
Philistia.

Maybe you've been asking God to give you a certain job, and
yet you don't have it. Maybe you've been praying for a home or
seeking God about the person you should marry. Perhaps you
want to go to school or get into a ministry, and yet all you seem
to do is go around in circles.

If this describes you, consider that you may not be ready for
God's answer. I can assure you, He is never in a hurry. Look at
Moses, the man at the head of Israel's exodus. God sent Moses
into the desert for forty years before calling him to liberate Israel.
God called the apostle Paul and then sent him down into Arabia
for a long period of solitude and study before turning him loose to
turn the world upside-down.

Too many of us are infected by the spirit of this age, which tells
us that unless we are out there doing and achieving something
every minute, we're losing out. But that is simply not true. The
record of God's Word is that He often takes His people on detours

to prepare them for usefulness. The important thing is not that you always know where God is taking you, but that you know *He* knows and you follow Him.

Finding the Light of His Guidance

Now we come to the good part, God's guiding light by which He faithfully led the Israelites. They may have been on a detour, but they weren't out there alone. The Bible says, "And the LORD went before them by day in a pillar of a cloud, to lead them the way; and by night in a pillar of fire, to give them light; to go by day and night: He took not away the pillar of the cloud by day, nor the pillar of fire by night, from before the people" (Exodus 13:21-22).

That pillar of cloud by day and the fire by night speaks of the Holy Spirit who guides us. After God redeems us, He sends His Spirit to guide us. On the night before Jesus' crucifixion, when He was about to leave His disciples and knew they would be in a panic, He promised to send them the Holy Spirit to be with them forever and to guide them (John 14:16; 16:13). Corrie ten Boom said, "There is no panic in heaven, only plans."

Just as the pillars of cloud and fire guided the Israelites in the wilderness, the Holy Spirit is your heaven-sent Guide in our detour through the wilderness. The important thing is that day by day, even moment by moment, we walk by the guidance of that pillar of cloud and of fire. The New Testament calls this walking in the Spirit.

Now as I said earlier, it is possible to be going around in circles because you are out of God's will. But you may also be in the very center of His will and still feel as if you are lost on a detour. But God knows exactly what He is doing with you.

Your job is to keep your eyes on the Lord Jesus Christ and to seek the inner witness of the Spirit that says, "This is the way. Walk in it."

You can obey the Lord's command with confidence because He sees things you cannot see. He knows the Philistines are out there. He knows the weaknesses you cannot see that need to be turned into strengths. Just keep your eyes on Him, and remember that God led Israel into the wilderness for a purpose. That's all you really need to know when you are undergoing the discipline of a detour.

THE DILEMMA OF DEAD ENDS

It's a wonderful feeling when a detour finally comes to an end and you are back on the main road, knowing exactly where you are and moving comfortably toward your destination. But it didn't happen that way for the Israelites, and so we find a second lesson to learn from their wanderings.

When You Are Hemmed in On Every Side

While Israel was moving through the wilderness, something was happening back in Egypt that would turn the discipline of Israel's detour into the dilemma of a dead end. "The LORD hardened the heart of Pharaoh king of Egypt" (Exodus 14:8). Old Pharaoh decided he had been a fool to let two million slaves go, and he mustered his massive army to pursue the Israelites and bring them back by force.

It wasn't hard for Pharaoh's fast-moving army to catch up with the Israelites. "All the horses and chariots of Pharaoh, and his horsemen, and his army . . . overtook them encamping by the sea, beside Pihahiroth, before Baalzephon" (v. 9). The people of Israel saw the Egyptians coming and became terrified when they saw the swords and shields of Pharaoh's army glinting in the sun.

Now God's people were still being led by His pillar of cloud and pillar of fire. But God's light had led them into a dead end, which is a lot worse than a detour. There were mountains on both sides of them, the Red Sea in front of them, and Pharaoh coming up behind them with blood in his eye. The Israelites were between the sword and the sea, hemmed in with no way out that they could see.

So they began to blame Moses as their aggravation turned to desperation. "And they said unto Moses, Because there were no graves in Egypt, hast thou taken us away to die in the wilderness? wherefore hast thou dealt thus with us, to carry us forth out of Egypt? Is not this the word that we did tell thee in Egypt, saying, Let us alone, that we may serve the Egyptians? For it had been better for us to serve the Egyptians, than that we should die in the wilderness" (Exodus 14:11-12).

The people were saying, "Moses, can't you read a map?" Map or no map, he was following the Lord. They were not there by happenstance. God had told Moses to camp at the very place where they were now pinned between Pharaoh and the Red Sea (Exodus 14:2). God led them there for a wonderful purpose, which He described in verse 3: "For Pharaoh will say of the children of Israel, They are entangled in the land, the wilderness hath shut them in."

Turning Our Desperation into Dependence on God

You see, God led the people into that dead end because He was going to bring judgment on Pharaoh, using the Israelites to bait

His hook. God said to Moses, "I will harden Pharaoh's heart, that he shall follow after them; and I will be honored upon Pharaoh, and upon all his host; that the Egyptians may know that I am the LORD" (v. 4).

In life we are going to encounter situations that are not just aggravating but push us right up against the wall. No one can avoid the dead ends. The Spanish have a proverb: "There is no home without its hush." This is true of God's children also. There are times when the light of God's guidance will lead you straight into a place of desperation, and you won't see any way out. There is no preacher who can give you a sermon to show you the way out, no book to help you, no doctor or banker to soothe your hurts. You are just there with no human way out.

Now remember that when you come to that place, there is still no panic in heaven, only plans. The Israelites weren't out of the will of God when they came to their dead end.

So why did God lead them there? He did it so that the place of desperation would become the place of dependence. When we see absolutely no way out, we have to cast ourselves completely upon the Lord. That is where He wants us, for then He can reveal His will to us.

God told the children of Israel what to do next. "And Moses said unto the people, Fear ye not, stand still, and see the salvation of the LORD, which he will show to you to day: for the Egyptians whom ye have seen to day, ye shall see them no more again for ever. The LORD shall fight for you, and ye shall hold your peace" (Exodus 14:13-14). And then when the people obeyed God, He told Moses, "Speak unto the children of Israel, that they go forward" (v. 15).

Four Things to Learn When You're at a Dead End

There are four wonderful rays of divine guidance in these verses that will help you make it through your dead end, even as the Israelites survived their dead-end experience in the wilderness.

1. *Don't be afraid.* The first thing Moses told the people was not to fear, even though they saw plenty of reasons to fear.

A dear preacher friend and man of God has blessed my heart many times. But I think he never blessed me more than he did a number of years ago when I talked to him one night in a hotel room after one of his sons had committed suicide. This boy had some mental problems caused by a severe chemical imbalance, and they had worked and worked with him. But over the Thanksgiving holidays on this particular year, my friend's precious boy died by his own hand.

This preacher's basic message for years has been the sufficiency of Jesus Christ. As I talked with him in that hotel room in the late hours of the night after this terrible tragedy, he said, "Adrian, I've learned one thing. There is nothing to fear. The reason I know that is I believe I've met the worst the devil can do, and Jesus is still sufficient."

My friend, I have not lost a child to suicide. But Joyce and I did lose a precious two-month-old baby boy to "crib death," and I can tell you with my friend that Christ is sufficient. I don't know how God will bring you to that place of desperation, but He wants you to know that you have nothing to fear because He is there with you.

Did you know that the words "Fear not" or their equivalent appear 365 times in the Bible? That's one for every day of the year. God's Word declares, "The Lord is my helper, and I will not fear what man shall do unto me" (Hebrews 13:6). God brings you to the place of desperation so that He might say to you, "Fear not."

2. *Stand still.* This is the second instruction Moses gave the Israelites. "Stand still, and see the salvation of the LORD, which he will show to you to day" (Exodus 14:13).

You cannot keep your feet still when your heart is racing with fear. The Bible says in Psalm 46:10, "Be still, and know that I am God." We're so busy manipulating and conniving, but finally we come to a place where God hems us in with the mountains around us, the sea in front of us, and the devil coming up behind. There is no place to run and nowhere to look but up. God tells us to stand still when we reach a dead end.

This advice is absolutely counter to the spirit of this age. I have a friend who said that when he was in management training for a restaurant, the boss told him that if he was on duty alone and there was a problem, he wanted my friend to do something, even if it was wrong. That's bad advice. It's always wrong to do wrong.

This reminds me of the story in Mark 5, when Jesus cast demons out of a man and sent them into a herd of two thousand pigs. The Bible says the entire herd rushed into the sea and drowned. Someone has said he can imagine one of those pigs saying to another, "Look, we're in a real mess, but whatever we do, let's stay together and keep moving."

That's the way many people think today. "We've got to do something!" But sometimes God puts us in a place where there is nothing we can do. And God tells us to just stand still. Don't just do something—stand there!

3. *See the Lord's salvation.* God wants us to stand still when we reach the dilemma of a dead end because He wants to show us His great salvation. Now I want you to notice something very important. Moses told the people to stand still and see God's salvation, their deliverance from Pharaoh, *before* it happened. They

were to see it with the eye of faith. It doesn't take much faith to thank God for delivering you when it's already been accomplished.

There is that time of faith when we simply say, "I refuse to fear. I stop and place myself, dear God, in Your hands. And, God, if You don't do it, it won't be done. And now by faith I see my way out, even when I don't see it."

4. *Move forward in faith.* Now notice something else. God did not act until the Israelites obeyed His word to cease their fear and stand still. After they had refocused their faith, He told them to move forward even as He commanded Moses to stretch out his rod over the Red Sea. "Speak unto the children of Israel, that they go forward."

Paul tells us that we serve a God who "calleth those things which be not as though they were" (Romans 4:17). Imitating our God, we by faith call things that are not as though they are, so that they might be. And when we do this, then God shows us a way out that we have never seen before.

There is no contradiction here between God's commands to stand still and to move forward. When we have come to that place of rest and confidence where by faith we see God in action, then we can move forward and reap the fruit of faith.

When the Israelites had learned the lessons of the dead end, God opened a way where there was no way before. God said to Moses, "Lift thou up thy rod, and stretch out thy hand over the sea, and divide it: and the children of Israel shall go on dry ground through the midst of the sea" (Exodus 14:16).

God turned that dead end into an eight-lane superhighway through the middle of the Red Sea. The Lord knows the way through the wilderness, and also through the sea. He knows a thousand ways to make a way for you. "I am the LORD, the God of all flesh: is there any thing too hard for me?" (Jeremiah 32:27). That so-called impossibility is God's opportunity to display His glory if you are following His guiding light in the pillar of cloud and pillar of fire.

THE DISAPPOINTMENT OF DRY HOLES

Now if detours and dead ends are difficult to deal with, look what happens when we run into the disappointment of dry holes. This was Israel's next stop on their wilderness journey.

God was still leading the people. They had not become lost or misread the map. But He led them in what seems to be a strange way. "So Moses brought Israel from the Rea sea, and they went out into the wilderness of Shur; and they went three days in the wilderness, and found no water" (Exodus 15:22).

Dry Holes Are Testing Places

Now this is a tough time. Imagine you've been driving all night looking for a motel on a remote stretch of highway, and you're bone-weary. And when you finally find a place, you get into your room and discover that there is no water. The tap is dry. That means no cold water to drink or hot water for a refreshing shower.

We've learned that if God led the Israelites on a detour and into a dead end for His purposes, He must have led them to this dry hole in the wilderness of Shur with a purpose in mind. Again, they were not there because they had sinned or displeased God. They were there because God had a test for them to take. We read about this test in the next verses of Exodus 15:

And when they came to Marah, they could not drink of the waters of Marah, for they were bitter: therefore the name of it

was called Marah [or bitter]. And the people murmured against Moses, saying, What shall we drink? And he cried unto the LORD; and the LORD showed him a tree, which when he had cast into the waters, the waters were made sweet: there he made for them a statute and an ordinance, and there he proved them.
—vv. 23-25, EMPHASIS ADDED

God "proved" the Israelites at Marah. That word literally means He tested them. When automakers develop a new model of car, they take it to a test track called a proving grounds to put it through the rigors of every road hazard and demanding driving condition imaginable. The carmaker does this to see if the new automobile will stand up to the demands of modern driving.

This is what God does with His people. His plan for the Israelites was described in retrospect in Deuteronomy 8:2, where Moses said, "Thou shalt remember all the way which the LORD thy God led thee these forty years in the wilderness, to humble thee, and to prove thee, to know what was in thine heart, whether thou wouldest keep his commandments, or no."

The Israelites did not arrive at that dry hole and place of bitter waters because God was angry with them or because Moses was a poor leader. It was a normal and natural part of their trip through the desert. The Lord was giving them a test to see what was in their hearts—not because He needed the information, but because they needed it.

God Has a Test Waiting for You

You are going to come to the same dry hole on occasion if you follow the Lord. This is quite a revelation to some believers. So many times we come to a dry place and say, "What went wrong?"

Nothing went wrong. God is on the throne, and He's leading

you. When you come to the disappointment of a dry hole, God is giving you a test.

How did Israel do on their test? They failed it miserably. We read above that the people murmured or complained against Moses. This is remarkable because Exodus 15:1-21 is the song of Moses that he and the people sang after God brought them through the Red Sea and destroyed Pharaoh's army.

Can you believe it? These people had just enjoyed a great victory, and they had sung and danced with joy. But just three days later they were murmuring and complaining. I'll tell you, you would think this was a modern church. In three days Moses had gone from hero to zero, and the people had gone from sweet songs to sour dispositions.

Are you a complainer when things don't go your way? I pray not, because there is something you need to learn about being a murmurer. Moses told the Israelites, "Your murmurings are not against us, but against the LORD" (Exodus 16:8).

The Terrible Sin of Complaining

Here is one of the greatest lessons you can ever learn. Teenagers who are murmuring about their parents need to know that God gave them those parents. People who complain about their teacher, pastor, or boss need to understand that God gave them those people to help and direct them. God gave Moses to the Israelites; so when they murmured against Moses, they were really griping against God.

Now let me put this on the lower shelf for you. Murmuring is a sin that God lists with such abominable transgressions as idolatry and fornication. In 1 Corinthians 10:1-13 Paul was warning his readers against imitating the sins of the Israelites in the wilderness.

Peruse those verses and you will find lust (v. 6), idolatry (v. 7), fornication (v. 8), tempting God (v. 9)—and murmuring. "Neither murmur ye, as some of them also murmured, and were destroyed of the destroyer" (v. 10).

With all that the Israelites had going for them in Moses' leadership and the light of God's guidance and presence, why did they complain? It was a lack of both faith and reason.

Let's be reasonable. Would God have brought the children of Israel through the Red Sea so wonderfully, only to bring them to a dry hole and let them die without water? That doesn't make sense.

Now I want to ask you a question. If Jesus Christ died for you on the cross and has saved you, do you think He saved you to abandon you? Do you think God has invested so much in you to let you go? That doesn't make sense (read Romans 8:32). Israel's complaining was rooted in unbelief, and it was a terrible sin against God. The water at Marah was bitter and undrinkable, and they thought they were going to die of thirst right there.

There are often two classes of people in the church: those who complain and those who know how to pray. The people murmured against Moses, but Moses went to the Lord. And God showed Moses a tree to throw into the waters and make them sweet.

God Always Has a Provision

What is interesting is that this tree had been there the whole time the Israelites were complaining. God had already made the provision, and He knew what He was going to do. That tree speaks of Jesus Christ, whom Jeremiah called the "righteous Branch" (Jeremiah 23:5). It also speaks of Calvary, for the Bible says in

1 Peter 2:24 that Jesus died upon a tree. God brought the people to this place of dryness and desperation so that He might display to them, by type and symbol, the sufficiency of Calvary and of the Lord Jesus Christ even in the barren places.

God tests us to prove us, so that we will learn Jesus is enough. So many times we come to the test of the dry hole, and what we don't realize is that God has a provision for us that may be right in front of us if we could only see it with the eyes of faith. I pray to God that you won't fail the test when it comes to you.

Here's something to file away in your mind and remember when God brings you to a dry place: Those grumbling Israelites couldn't see it from where they were, but just over the hill from Marah was a beautiful oasis. "They came to Elim, where were twelve wells of water, and threescore and ten palm trees: and they encamped there by the waters" (Exodus 15:27).

Isn't that amazing? The people left Marah and ran right into Elim. One day they were complaining that God had forsaken them, and before they knew it they were resting in a lush oasis.

No matter how dry the place, God has a provision. I remember hearing a remarkable example of this in the life of Aleksandr Solzhenitsyn, the famous Russian Christian and author of *The Gulag Archipelago*, the gripping account of his ordeal in a Soviet Communist prison camp.

Solzhenitsyn said that when he was suddenly arrested by Stalin's secret police and sent to a labor camp in Siberia, he was so tortured in mind and body that he contemplated suicide. He wondered if anyone in the world knew where he was, and he felt utterly alone. He drew up a suicide plan in his mind, telling no one of his intention.

But the day Solzhenitsyn was planning to take his own life,

he was sitting on the ground when another prisoner walked by and looked at him. It was as if this man saw into Solzhenitsyn's mind and heart and knew he was desperate. The prisoners were not allowed to speak, but the man knelt down in front of Solzhenitsyn and drew a cross in the dirt.

Solzhenitsyn said he drew new strength from this man's simple reminder of the hope we have in Christ—and within a week, he was a free man in Geneva, Switzerland! It turned out that people around the world had been praying for Aleksandr Solzhenitsyn and petitioning for his release. "To think that I was about to commit suicide," he said later, "and within a week I was free!"

You may be camped beside a dry hole right now, wondering why God has forsaken you. God hasn't forsaken you, my friend. He is proving you. He brought you to that dry place. It's right on the map He has drawn for your life. So don't complain. Calvary is sufficient for you. Right over the hill God has an oasis. You can't see it, but God can see it.

The important thing in life is not that you know what God knows. That will never happen. The important thing for you is to keep following God's light, the pillars of cloud and of fire.

In New Testament terms, walk in the Spirit. And if you have to take a detour, praise God. If you come to a dead end, praise God. If you come to a dry hole, praise God. Your Lord knows the way through the wilderness, as the old gospel chorus says. "All I have to do is follow."

3

Walking in Light
A Formula for Fellowship

When I was a young preacher, I pastored a small church in a little Florida town on the edge of the famous Everglades. It was a joy for Joyce and me to serve the Lord in that church, and we met some wonderful people, including a deacon who hunted frogs for a living. He was a professional frogger. He would go out at night in an airboat and gig frogs, and he made a nice living from it.

This man once told me a story I have never forgotten. It seems that before he was saved, he used to poach alligators as well as hunt frogs. He told me a big alligator's hide was worth far more than he could ever make hunting frogs in one night. He and his buddies couldn't shoot the alligators for fear of alerting the game warden; so they would shine a very powerful light beam in the gator's eyes as they eased alongside him in the boat. The beam would keep the alligator on the surface of the water until the boat got close enough for my friend to swing a big hammer and hit the gator between the eyes.

Well, he told me that one night he spotted the biggest alligator he had ever seen. He knew this gator would be valuable, and he didn't want to miss him; so he idled the motor on his boat and came up right alongside the alligator. This man, who is small and wiry, gave his heavy hammer a mighty swing, but he missed the gator, and the force of the hammer coming all the way around flipped him out of the boat. He landed right on top of the alligator, straddling that huge beast with his legs. "Pastor," he said, "I got back in the boat without even getting wet!"

I've thought about that story many times, and what comes through to me is that as Christians we should react to sin the way my former deacon reacted to landing on top of that alligator. A Christian can slip and fall into sin, but I believe a true child of God will fear sin as much as that man feared that alligator. We may fall, but we will desire to make a quick recovery, just as my friend in Florida did so long ago.

It's the recovery from sin for believers that I want to address in this chapter as we learn what it means to walk in light. What happens when you slip and fall and find yourself straddling an alligator called sin? How do get back in the boat as quickly as possible so fellowship with God is restored?

THE ESSENTIALS OF FELLOWSHIP WITH GOD

This is the subject the apostle John speaks to in the first chapter of his first epistle. John says his purpose is to tell us how to enjoy fellowship with one another and with God the Father and God the Son. "That which we have seen and heard declare we unto you, that ye also may have fellowship with us: and truly our fellowship is with the Father, and with his Son Jesus Christ. And these things write we unto you, that your joy may be full" (1 John 1:3-4). The path to fullness of joy lies in fellowship.

Set Your Sights on the Standard

Now having revealed his purpose, John proceeds to tell us how we can experience unhindered fellowship with the Lord. The standard for this is the holiness and purity of His light: "This then is the message which we have heard of him, and declare unto you, that God is light, and in him is no darkness at all. If we say that we have fellowship with him, and walk in darkness, we lie, and do not the truth: But if we walk in the light, as he is in the light, we have fellowship one with another, and the blood of Jesus Christ his Son cleanseth us from all sin" (vv. 5-7).

We have talked about the absolute purity of light, how it is unaffected by anything it shines upon or passes through. If we are going to walk with God, John says, we must walk in the light because God does not operate in the darkness in terms of His relationship with His children.

Name Sin for What It Really Is

The world tries to call sin everything but what it is—rebellion and disobedience against God that brings His judgment. But we cannot deny or ignore the reality of sin as believers and expect to live in joyful, unbroken fellowship with God. In fact, the Bible says that anyone who claims he doesn't sin is a liar. John writes: "If we say that we have no sin, we deceive ourselves, and the truth is not in us" (1 John 1:8).

We need to understand the nature of sin because God only forgives sin. He doesn't forgive mistakes. Now don't misunderstand. I am not saying God judges or condemns us for our mistakes. He will discipline and instruct us for our mistakes. But if we insist on calling our sins mistakes, we will never deal with them.

A mistake is taking the wrong exit on the freeway or forgetting to put the trash out. But when a person commits adultery or steals from his employer and then says, "I made a mistake," that is a dodge for the real issue of a sinful heart. If you don't see sin as an affront to a holy God but call it by some other name—a misjudgment, malfunction, or sickness—then you can say that man is ill but not evil. He's weak but not wicked. He's sick but not sinful.

The problem is that even though our society uses these terms for sin, we all still bear a burden of guilt because the image of God is stamped on our soul. The world's dilemma is that people are carrying a heavy burden of guilt for which they need cleansing, but they lack a sense of sin that drives them to seek cleansing. So they search for relief in all the wrong places. They see themselves needing to get their thinking straight or fix a mistake when they really need forgiveness and cleansing from God.

Now if the evolutionist is right and human beings are the product of blind forces working over aeons of time, then there is no such thing as sin because there is no God to whom we are accountable. To the evolutionist, what we call sin is just an accident or a slight stumble as man progresses upward from the primordial soup in which life spontaneously began.

Well, I don't know if evolutionists study history or read the newspaper, but if the human race is progressing upward from the soup, then we have gone from soup to nuts. We are not progressing at all. Mankind began in perfection, made in the image of God, but sin has ruined the race. But evolution allows for no category called sin.

The educator says the solution for our flaws is not time but learning. If that were true, then the most knowledgeable people among us would be the least sinful. Apply that theory to human history, however, and you soon arrive at Nazi Germany. There was probably not a nation in the world that had a higher level of education than Germany when Hitler and the Nazis took over.

When I was in college, I took a course in philosophy from a professor who also taught me Greek. I admired this man deeply and listened to him with awe as he taught from the store of his great learning. But one day this brilliant professor went out to a lonely place, spread some newspapers on the ground, and then put a pistol to his temple and took his own life. Education was not the answer to life for him.

Then there is science, which tells us that mankind's problem is just defective genes, which we can manipulate and eliminate by genetic engineering. In other words, if we could just marry Superman to the Bionic Woman, then maybe somehow we could deal with human flaws. But again, if science were the answer, then the most gifted, good-looking, and strongest among us would have the least problem with sin. But in many cases, the exact opposite is true.

The sociologist tells us the problem with humans is environmental. We have had a lot of experience with this one, because our nation spent the sixties and seventies trying to eliminate poverty and crime by putting people in better housing and giving them money and jobs.

That experiment to produce the "Great Society" was a dismal failure. In fact, the recent scandals at the very top of corporate America prove that people in the very best environment humanly possible have not escaped the sin problem.

And of course we cannot talk about faulty views of sin without including the psychologist and the psychiatrist. These experts do their best to remove people's feelings of guilt by telling them those feelings have no basis in reality.

All of these views fall short of accounting for sin. The blood of Jesus Christ is the only answer to the sin problem. We must realize this if we are to live in fellowship with God.

GOD FORGIVES AND FORGETS OUR SIN

The heart of this chapter is the promise of 1 John 1:9 that God will cleanse us of sin to restore our fellowship with Him. God cleanses sin, and here's the wonderful part: God forgets the sin He cleanses. Before we look at this great verse, which is addressed to believers, it's important that we understand what God does with our sins when we are saved.

God declares, "Their sins and their iniquities will I remember no more" (Hebrews 8:12). In Isaiah 43:25 the Lord says, "I, even I, am he that blotteth out thy transgressions for mine own sake, and will not remember thy sins." Over and over again God tells us He has buried our sin in the grave of His forgetfulness.

Now that doesn't mean God forgets our sin intellectually or that it slips from His memory. God could never learn or forget anything because then He would be less than God. His knowledge is infinite, and nothing escapes Him.

God cannot lose or gain any knowledge. So when the Bible says He forgets our sins, it means that He treats them as forgiven sins. He does not hold our sins against us anymore. God does not remember our sin simply as sin but as *forgiven* sin, and there's an eternity of difference between the two.

Now let me tell you something wonderful. You may not be able to forget your sins. But if God remembers them as forgiven sins, then you can remember them the same way. You may remember a time when you told a lie or were filled with pride. I can remember sins I have committed—but thank God, I can remember them as forgiven sins. I don't want to dig up what God has buried.

I'm making a point of this because we need to learn the difference between the forgiveness that puts us into the family of God and the forgiveness that the apostle John speaks of in 1 John 1. When you come to the Lord Jesus Christ and are born again, all of your sins—past, present, and future—are forgiven. God will never lay those sins to your charge. "Blessed is the man to whom the Lord will not impute [or charge] sin" (Romans 4:8).

I hope you know that if God were to charge one half of one penny against your account and mine, we would still be lost sinners on our way to hell. But praise God, He has forgiven us. Our past is forgiven, and our future is as secure as the Person and the promises of God.

The Difference Between Sonship and Fellowship

Now having said that, I want to go back to 1 John 1 and look very carefully at the difference between our sonship and our fellowship. We read verses 6-7 earlier, but let's consider them again in this context: "If we say that we have fellowship with him, and walk in darkness, we lie, and do not the truth: But if we walk in the light, as he is in the light, we have fellowship one with another, and the blood of Jesus Christ his Son cleanseth us from all sin."

We just finished talking about how God buries our sins and will never bring them up again, and now John is discussing the issue of sin in a believer's life. But this is a different issue, because every child of God knows Him in two ways. We know Him through sonship when we are born into His family and He becomes our heavenly Father. But we also know God through fellowship as we live in His presence each day.

When I was born into the family of God, my standing as His son was settled forever. I can never be unborn as a son of God, just as I can never be unborn as a member of the Rogers family. No matter what I do, I will always be my Father's child. That is sonship, and it is for all eternity. Nothing can change that moment when I was born again by the Spirit of God and became a member of God's family.

But my fellowship with God at any given time is another matter. Theologians call this our state, meaning our current condition before God, as opposed to our standing, which is our eternal, unchanging sonship. My father never denied me, but there were times when he would tell me to cut the grass or clean out the garage, and I didn't do it. Or I would do something he specifically told me not to do.

On those occasions when I was disobedient, my fellowship with my dad changed dramatically! He knew how to apply the board of education to the seat of knowledge. I would get the spanking that I so richly deserved. It hurt, and it was supposed to hurt, because my father wanted to teach me the pain of disobedience and guide me in the right path. The Bible says, "Now no chastening for the present seemeth to be joyous, but grievous: nevertheless afterward it yieldeth the peaceable fruit of righteousness unto them which are exercised thereby" (Hebrews 12:11).

My father never said, "You're no son of mine" when I acted up. He disciplined me to bring me back into fellowship with him. And he didn't keep spanking me for the same sin. The tears were followed by the "peaceable fruit" of restored fellowship with my father. If you're a parent, you know what it is to hold and hug your child after discipline to reassure that child of your love.

Fellowship Can Be Interrupted by Sin

Now I hope you get the point that sin interrupts our fellowship with God. When John speaks of our walking in the light as opposed to walking in darkness, he's not referring to being saved or lost. The light here is the light of God's favor and blessing that shines on us when we are living in open, unhindered fellowship with Him. The only thing that can block this light is our sin, but God has made provision for our forgiveness and cleansing so that His full light can shine on us.

HOW TO WALK IN THE LIGHT

Remember how wonderful it is when you are in the darkness to have the light flood in upon you and illuminate everything so you can see where you're going? God wants His children to live day by day, and even moment by moment, flooded with the light of His fellowship. When you stumble and fall into sin, God has made a way for you to be cleansed so that you are not walking in the darkness, but in His marvelous light. Let me give you three wonderful truths from 1 John so that, if you heed them, you can walk in the light as a way of life.

Sin Must Be Exposed to the Light

We just learned that we cannot say we are in fellowship with God and yet live in the darkness of unconfessed sin. Our sin must be brought into the light of God's holiness and purity.

I want you to notice something very interesting in John's epistle. The phrase "If we say" is repeated three times (vv. 6, 8, 10). Each one of these verses begins with that little trinity of words, "If we say."

John is talking about people who try to deny their sin rather than exposing it to God's searchlight. These verses are interesting because they reveal the downward path we take when we lie about the presence of sin in our lives that the Holy Spirit wants to bring into the light. Let me show you what I mean.

The first step downward for a child of God who denies his or her sin is that this person *begins to lie to other people.* "If we say that we have fellowship with him, and walk in darkness, we lie, and do not the truth" (1 John 1:6). To whom are we saying this when it is not true? We are saying it to other believers, both by our words and our actions.

What happens is that a believer who is allowing sin to build up and linger in his heart comes to church on Sunday and sings about God's love and forgiveness with everyone else, even when he knows his heart isn't right. That's a form of lying. He studies the Bible in Sunday school and says, "Amen" to the sermon. Later people meet him and ask, "How are you doing, brother?" And he answers, "Just fine. Praise the Lord." And everyone assumes this brother is walking in victory.

I think all of us have experienced times like this. We know our heart isn't right, but we don't want the person next to us to know it. We don't want to admit to our spouse that we are harboring sin and need to be cleansed; so we act as if everything is fine. We deny our sin by lying to others.

If we don't stop it there, we soon take the second step downward. *We start lying to ourselves:* "If we say that we have no sin, we deceive ourselves, and the truth is not in us" (1 John 1:8).

Tell any lie long enough, and you'll start believing it yourself. You will begin to give yourself more slack to allow for your sin and thus deceive yourself into thinking it really isn't so bad after all. A person in this condition is a spiritual schizophrenic. It's the path to depression.

But there's a third step downward on this descent into deception, and this is the most serious step of all. "If we say that we have not sinned, we make him [God] a liar, and his word is not in us" (1 John 1:10). *We end up lying to God.* If God the Holy Spirit says something is a sin and we deny it, we are calling God a liar. The most dangerous thing we can do is to try to conceal our sin from God.

What we need to do is bring our sin into the light. Notice what happens when we do this. The Bible does not say that when we come to God with our sin, we are condemned and browbeaten. The promise is that if we will come into the light, we will enjoy fellowship with God. My purpose in writing this is not to make you feel bad, but to show you how you can be absolutely, totally, and wonderfully cleansed from all unrighteousness.

Light reveals what is wrong. The closer you get to a bright light, the more imperfections show up in any object. If you want to know whether there is any sin in your heart and life today, just step into God's light by praying as David prayed: "Search me, O God, and know my heart: try me, and know my thoughts: and see if there be any wicked way in me" (Psalm 139:23-24). Ask God to shine the searchlight of His holiness into your heart.

When you do that, the Holy Spirit will be faithful to convict you of any sin that will ruin your fellowship with God and with other believers. You don't have to do morbid introspection. The Holy Spirit will deal with sin that is present, and the purpose of

His conviction is not to make you feel bad, but to bring you to confession, repentance, and restored fellowship.

Now I want to make a distinction here that is crucial to this matter of walking in the light. There is a vast difference between the Holy Spirit's conviction and Satan's accusation. You need to understand this because the Holy Spirit is not the only one who will bring up your sin. The devil will bring up your sin also, but with a completely different purpose in mind. I see three vital contrasts between the Holy Spirit's work and the devil's schemes.

First of all, the Holy Spirit convicts you *legitimately*. He will address the sin in your life that has not yet been confessed and cleansed, not dredge up things from the past that are under the blood of Christ. But the devil's accusations are illegitimate because he will bring back to your remembrance that which God has forgiven and forgotten, in order to keep you in guilt and bondage.

Suppose you tell a lie, and the Holy Spirit convicts you of that sin. You confess it, telling God you are sorry and asking Him to forgive and cleanse you. What has happened to that sin? As far as God is concerned, it is gone forever. So if that sin comes up again to torment you, it is the devil accusing you.

That's his specialty. The Bible calls the devil the accuser of the brethren (Revelation 12:10). Satan accuses you before God and before your own conscience. He will bring up not only that one sin, but every sin he can find to torment you with guilt.

The devil is cruel, because before you sin he will tell you, "Go ahead and do it. You can get away with it." But then after you sin, he will say, "You shouldn't have done that. You call yourself a Christian and you do things like that?" He leads you into sin, and then he accuses you for doing what he led you into doing.

But the Holy Spirit's conviction is diametrically opposed to Satan's accusations. His searchlight always exposes sin and leads you to seek confession and cleansing. Now if you refuse to confess that sin and then try to have fellowship with God, you will indeed be miserable. But the purpose of that misery is to bring about "godly sorrow [which] worketh repentance" (2 Corinthians 7:10).

A second characteristic of the Holy Spirit's conviction is that He will convict you *specifically*. He is like a skilled physician who presses right on the sore spot. We say, "Oh, that hurt." There is a reason for the pain. That's where the sin is, and the Holy Spirit will call it by name. Don't try to deal with sin by saying, "O God, if I have sinned in any way, forgive me."

Praying like that is a waste of breath. Say, "Lord, I told a lie. Forgive me." Or "I confess that I was cruel to my wife. Please forgive me." When you name your sin specifically, that's where you are forgiven.

You may ask, "Adrian, can I really know what specific sins to confess? Does the Holy Spirit actually get that specific?" Yes, He does, and yes, you can. Come on, let's be honest. You and I usually know when we have done something wrong. We apologize to those we have hurt or offended, and God wants to hear the same specific confession from us.

But when the devil accuses you, if he can't find some specific sin to throw in your face, he will accuse you in a general way. He'll come with oppressive thoughts: "You're no good. Forget trying to serve God. You'll never make it. You have a vile, sinful nature. God couldn't love anybody like you."

A lot of Christians live under the oppression of the devil because they have not learned to answer Satan's lies with the truth of God's Word. Jesus answered the devil three times in the wilderness, "It is written" (Matthew 4:1-11).

So when the devil tries to condemn you, show him Romans 8:1: "There is therefore now no condemnation to them which are in Christ Jesus, who walk not after the flesh, but after the Spirit." And for good measure throw in 2 Peter 1:4, which says you have become a partaker of the divine nature. You are no longer who you used to be in Adam. You are now in Christ.

The devil doesn't want you to understand this. Unlike a physician who wants to find the pain and heal it, the devil is like a virus. He wants to make you feel bad all over. If you are feeling terrible and don't know why, that is the devil. The Holy Spirit will only convict you of sin that has not been confessed, and He will tell you exactly what it is. He'll put a name, a face, a time, and a date on it.

Not only does the Holy Spirit convict you legitimately and specifically, but *redemptively*. That is, the Holy Spirit's purpose in convicting you is to restore you to intimate fellowship with God. When God deals with you as a son or daughter, He's not trying to get even with you or break you down. He hates it when your fellowship with Him is broken; so He wants to bring you back. The promise of Scripture is that confessed sin will be forgiven.

But the devil accuses you destructively. The Spirit wants you to draw you toward God, while the devil wants to drive you to despair and away from God. His accusations are designed to tear you down and destroy your Christian walk and witness.

But all you need to do is open your heart to the Holy Spirit, who will reveal any unconfessed, unforsaken, and unforgiven sin in your life. Then you are ready to do something with that sin.

Sin Must Be Expressed to the Lord

When the Holy Spirit exposes your sin to the light, then it must be expressed to the Lord. Now we come to the familiar words of 1 John 1:9, where the apostle writes: "If we confess our sins, he is faithful and just to forgive us our sins, and to cleanse us from all unrighteousness."

What does it mean to confess your sin? The Greek word for "confess" helps us here because it means "to say the same thing," or to agree. A confession of sin is not just admission of sin. It is agreement with God about the awfulness of that sin and your need for forgiveness. To confess your sin is to name it and nail it to the cross. When the Holy Spirit calls something sin, say, "Lord, I agree. This is sin, and I confess it to You and claim Your promise of cleansing."

How do you confess your sin? Let me give you three ways that are drawn from our text. The first is *immediately*, as soon as the Spirit makes you aware of it. The word "confess" in 1 John 1:9 is in the present tense, meaning a continuous action. Don't save up all of your sins until the end of the day, or even worse until the end of the week. Confession calls for immediate action.

When you get a speck of dust in your eye or a sharp splinter in your finger, you don't ignore it and say, "I think I'll get that out later tonight before I go to bed, or maybe I'll wait until this Sunday at church." Of course not. You deal with the irritant immediately. That's what God wants you to do with your sin. Confess it immediately. And you can do it anywhere and at any time. "Lord, what I just said was wrong. Forgive me, and cleanse me."

So many of us ride a spiritual roller coaster simply because we have not learned the simple but life-changing truth of how to deal with sin. We come to church on a low note, but then we hear and sing God's Word, confess our sins and get right with Him, and zoom to the top of the roller coaster. We go along the top for a time, but then something happens, and we plunge to the bottom again. And you know what happens when a roller coaster hits bottom. It has to make a long, slow climb back to the top again.

But the Christian life was not designed to be a roller coaster. The Bible commands us, "Be filled with the Spirit" (Ephesians 5:18), and the language there means that the Spirit-filled life is to be our moment-by-moment experience. How can we maintain this kind of consistent walk with God? One way is by immediate confession of sin. Don't ride a sin all the way to the bottom before you own it and confess it.

Second, confess your sin *specifically*, just as the Holy Spirit convicts you. The word "sins" in 1 John 1:9 is plural, suggesting that individual sins are in view, not sin as a general category. We have already talked about the importance of naming the sins that the Spirit brings to our attention. We sing the song "Count your many blessings, name them one by one. And it will surprise you what the Lord has done." Maybe we should also sing, "Count your many sins, name them one by one. And it will surprise you what *you* have done"!

Third, confess your sins *confidently*. The confidence is in our God, who is "faithful and just to forgive us our sins." If God did not cleanse and forgive you when you confessed your sins to Him, He would be unfaithful and unjust. But that would be totally contrary to His character. Jesus shed His blood for those sins to save you and keep you absolutely, wonderfully, and totally cleansed before God.

What a wonderful way to live. There is nothing more exhilarating than being clean in God's sight. Do you remember the mouthwash commercial in which a husband and wife start to say hello and kiss each other first thing in the morning, but then cover their mouths and run into the bathroom because they both have morning breath? But when they use the right brand of mouthwash, their mouths feel tingly clean, and they kiss each other with relish.

That feeling of being tingly clean you get when you clean your mouth is the feeling you can have all over when God cleanses you of all sin and you know you are right with Him.

My friend, God wants to show you His love today. If you are out of fellowship with Him in any way, I urge you to lay this book down and seek Him right now. The Holy Spirit is waiting for you, and God will be faithful to forgive you. There is no reason to wait.

Sin Must Be Expelled from the Life

Make no mistake about it. John has not written these wonderful words about God's faithfulness to forgive in order to encourage us to sin, but to encourage us not to sin. God's wonderful forgiveness and overmastering love are not a license to sin, but an encouragement to holiness. Notice how the apostle opens the second chapter of his epistle:

> *My little children, these things write I unto you, that ye sin not. And if any man sin, we have an advocate with the Father, Jesus Christ the righteous: And he is the propitiation for our sins: and not for ours only, but also for the sins of the whole world. And hereby we do know that we know him, if we keep his commandments. He that saith, I know him, and keepeth not his commandments, is a liar, and the truth is not in him.*

But whoso keepeth his word, in him verily is the love of God perfected: hereby know we that we are in him. He that saith he abideth in him ought himself also so to walk, even as he walked.
—1 JOHN 2:1-6

Here John speaks of an advocate, a special word for a lawyer. An advocate is a person who takes your side and pleads your case because he has your best interests at heart. The Lord Jesus Christ is our defense attorney when we fail. At the righteous throne of God He pleads for us the propitiation or saving sacrifice of His blood. God the Father has accepted this sacrifice and is completely propitiated, or satisfied, by Jesus' blood. This is how God can be faithful and just to forgive us.

But notice that our lawyer who is our propitiation is also "Jesus Christ the righteous." His nature is righteousness, and His desire is that sin will be expelled from our lives. To be like Christ means that we want to be righteous as He is righteous.

Some may believe that God's willingness to forgive means that we can sin all we want to. It may surprise you to know that I sin all I want to—because I don't want to! Nothing would please me more than to never sin again.

I like the way someone has described what the difference should be in our attitude toward sin before and after we know Christ. Before we knew Christ, we used to leap into sin and love it. Now we lapse into sin and loathe it. May that ever be the attitude of our hearts. The person who knows Jesus Christ the righteous wants sin to be expelled from his life.

4

The Discipline of Darkness

What to Do When the Lights Go Out

One of the hymns that God's people have been singing for almost a century is "He Keeps Me Singing." This joy-filled song of praise begins, "There's within my heart a melody, Jesus whispers sweet and low." You can't sing this wonderful song without your heart being lifted.

But did you know that this song was born in the deepest darkness you can imagine? The author of both the words and music was a pastor and evangelist from Georgia named Luther Bridgers. He is said to have written "He Keeps Me Singing" after his wife and three sons died in a fire while he was away holding revival meetings in Kentucky.

It is wonderful to talk about the light of God and the joy of living in His presence and in warm fellowship with the Savior. But what happens when the lights go out and we find ourselves surrounded by darkness? Does the darkness mean that God is displeased with us? Or does He have something to teach us that can only be learned in the darkness?

I want you to know, dear friend, that when we come to those times in our lives when the lights seem to go out and we are plunged into darkness, God is with us. Darkness and light are alike to Him. The testimony of Luther Bridgers and the saints of all the ages is that God is there in the darkness just as He is in the light, loving and sustaining us and drawing us closer to Himself.

As a pastor I am often called in a time of calamity, and the first question that is usually asked is, "Pastor, why did God let this happen?" That's a natural question because we need for things to makes sense, especially in a time of loss. As one writer said, we can bear the *what* of almost anything if we can just know the *why*.

But the why of a particular calamity is seldom easily discovered, and it may never be known. It is not ours to ask why, for the whys belong to God. The question we need to ask when the lights go out is *how*. How are we going to respond to those circumstances God has placed us in that seem to make no sense? This is the question of faith.

We might as well admit it: Christians are often left in the dark when it comes to life's circumstances. Even as you read this book you may be going through financial distress or enduring misrepresentation and disgrace. You may have a broken heart because of a broken home. You may even be at the deathbed of a child.

When these things come upon us, the question haunts us: Why? I cannot answer the why of your trial, but I have five observations or propositions I want to lay on your heart that will help you find your way back from despair and confusion when the lights go out.

THOSE OF GREATEST DEVOTION MAY KNOW THE DEEPEST DARKNESS

One of the paradoxes of the Christian life is that the believers who are closest to the Lord and know Him in the sweetest intimacy are usually those who have come through the deepest trials. They have learned that walking with God and obeying Him are not a guarantee against calamity or pain.

The prophet Isaiah said, "Who is among you that feareth the LORD, that obeyeth the voice of his servant, that walketh in darkness, and *hath no light*? let him trust in the name of the LORD, and stay upon his God" (Isaiah 50:10, emphasis added). It is possible to fear the Lord and obey Him, and yet walk in darkness. But we are also going to learn that God's Word has some wise counsel for us in these times.

Days of darkness are not unusual, even for God's choicest saints. No matter how close we walk to the Lord, it is not always sweetness and light. We need not get the distorted idea that if we give our lives to Jesus all will be joy and light and we will walk a rose-petaled path to heaven. That is often the promise that is made, especially if you listen to the "health and wealth" preachers on television. Their theology allows no place for suffering or loss.

But the testimony of the Bible and of others is that we are not going to waltz through life in a crescendo of health and success, then relax in a serene old age and make a glorious exit. Thousands of believers who love God are deeply perplexed and in darkness today. There comes a time when the lights go out, heaven is silent, and nothing seems to make sense.

Think of some of the Bible's greatest saints. Job was a godly man, and yet he was perplexed by the trials that befell him as he lost his family and everything he owned. Job cried out, "He hath fenced up my way that I cannot pass, and he hath set darkness in my paths" (Job 19:8).

The prophet Jeremiah was chosen of the Lord to deliver

His message; yet Jeremiah struggled with the burden of speaking to a disobedient people who not only rejected God's warnings but beat and imprisoned His prophet. Jeremiah was known as "the weeping prophet" because of his anguish: "Oh that my head were waters, and mine eyes a fountain of tears, that I might weep day and night for the slain of the daughter of my people!" (Jeremiah 9:1).

Turning to the New Testament we find another prophet, John the Baptist, languishing in prison for faithfully proclaiming God's Word. It did not make sense to John that Jesus could work miracles—even raise the dead—and yet he, John, was in prison. He became perplexed and sent messengers to Jesus to ask, "Art thou he that should come? or look we for another?" (Luke 7:19).

Even the great apostle Paul, mighty in faith, knew times of deep perplexity and suffering. He wrote: "We are troubled on every side, yet not distressed; we are perplexed, but not in despair; persecuted, but not forsaken; cast down, but not destroyed" (2 Corinthians 4:8-9). Earlier he had written of troubles so pressing that "we despaired even of life" (2 Corinthians 1:8).

Not only these people of the Bible, but the great Christians of history have had the same experience of suffering and distress. Many of them spoke of a dark night of the soul when comfort flees and the lights seem to go out.

So if you are in darkness, at least you may be in good company. Darkness does not necessarily mean that you have sinned or that you are out of the will of God. Notice in Isaiah 50:10 that God is speaking of the person who fears Him and obeys the voice of His servant. This is the one who is in darkness.

THE FAITH THAT IS BORN IN THE LIGHT OFTEN GROWS BEST IN THE DARKNESS

One reason God either leads us into the darkness or allows us to enter it is that He has something more in mind for us than our ease and comfort. It is in the darkness that we are forced to trust the Lord and lean upon Him in a way we would never do if every day were easy.

You can test this yourself. When have you grown the most spiritually in your Christian life? Was it in the happy, sunny days when everything seemed perfect, or at midnight when you wept out your tears and cried in the darkness to God over a wayward child or a bad report from the doctor? We grow best in the darkness because it is there that we seek God as at no other time in our lives.

I love the little poem "Along the Road," written by Robert Browning Hamilton, which says: "I walked a mile with Pleasure, she chattered all the way. But left me none the wiser for all she had to say. I walked a mile with Sorrow, and ne'er a word said she. But oh, the things I learned from her, when Sorrow walked with me!"

Faith, like film, is developed in the dark. Human nature is such that if we were never tested, few of us would have the motivation to pursue God no matter what the cost. He wants us to develop a strong faith, a faith that goes beyond our understanding and experience. A wise man once said that we should never doubt in the dark what God has shown us in the light. In God's school of faith He reveals His truth and His promises to us, and then He puts us in the crucible so that we might learn that what we know in our heads and hearts is really true.

The real test of your faith is how you act in the dark. Anyone can sing praises to God and testify of His goodness when the money is flowing, the health is good, and everything is looking up. But when the light turns to darkness, then we discover what our faith is made of and where our trust really lies. What should you do when the lights suddenly go out in your life? Let me give you three principles from Isaiah 50:10.

First, *look to the Lord*. According to this great verse, we are to "trust in the name of the LORD." Warren Wiersbe said, "We live by promises, and not by explanations." Just because things do not make sense to you does not mean they do not make sense. And just because they do not make sense now does not mean that they will not make sense someday. Faith begins where our reason and explanations end. Trust the Lord when things don't seem to add up and you are perplexed.

Second, *obey the Lord*. We have seen in Isaiah 50:10 that the person in darkness is one who obeys God. Don't stop obeying what you know is God's will even when the darkness closes around you. Don't stop praying, for example. Your prayers don't have to be flowery or theologically astute. You have a great High Priest, the Lord Jesus Christ, who is interceding for you in heaven. It is His worth and not your words that matter.

Don't stop witnessing, even if no one seems to respond. Don't stop serving the Lord and His people. You may be the person who is needed to help bring another believer through the darkness. Don't stop giving even in the middle of a financial reversal. Don't stop praising God even if you don't feel like praising Him. Obey God in the dark, and He will lead you back to the light.

Third, *lean upon the Lord*. The word "stay" in Isaiah 50:10 means to lean upon for support. This verb is the root of the word translated "staff." Just as a shepherd leans on his staff, you should lean upon the Lord. In Psalm 23:4 David wrote, "Yea, though I walk through the valley of the shadow of death, I will fear no evil: for thou art with me; thy rod and thy staff they comfort me." It is better to be in a dark valley and leaning on Jesus than to be on a sunlit mountain without Him.

We may not understand what is happening to us, but our relationship with God is more important than a list of reasons. It may be that we do not know *why* in order that we may know *who*. I believe that even if the Lord were to give us all the reasons for what He does, many of us still wouldn't understand it all or be satisfied. So God gives us something much better than reasons and explanations. He gives us Himself.

David came to understand the difference between reason and relationship. Notice that in Psalm 23 he went from talking about the Lord ("The LORD is my shepherd," v. 1) to talking with the Lord ("Thou art with me; thy rod and thy staff they comfort me," v. 4). What made the difference? David was in the dark valley, and he discovered that God was there with him. No matter how dark life becomes, you will find Jesus standing somewhere in the shadows. The darkness may hide, but it cannot divide.

We mentioned Job earlier and the way this righteous man suffered. Job became so perplexed in the midst of his suffering that he wanted to argue with God. "God, you owe me some answers!" he said in effect. But read Job 38—42, and you'll see that Job never got any answers. What he got, however, was so much better. He learned that God alone was enough. "I have heard of thee by the hearing of the ear: but now mine eye seeth thee" (Job 42:5).

Most Christians believe that God is necessary. But sometimes God may put us into the darkness to learn that He is not only necessary, but all that we need. Someone has said you will never learn that God is all you need until He is all you have. Faith grows strongest in the darkness.

SOME THINGS ARE SEEN IN THE DARKNESS THAT CANNOT BE SEEN IN THE LIGHT

Another truth we need to remember when we are in the darkness is that there is more to see in the dark than first meets the eye.

This is not a contradictory statement, but a fact. You know that when you first step from bright sunlight into a dark room, you can't see anything. But as your eyes adjust, you begin to make out shapes and forms, and you can see what is in the room.

In the days before the army had all of its infrared equipment that allows soldiers to see in the dark, they were trained to protect their night vision. The drill sergeants would take the soldiers out on training and stay out until the sun had gone down and darkness set in. The soldiers would be able to see because their eyes had had time to adjust to the darkness.

But they were told that a sudden burst of light, such as would happen in warfare, could cause their eyes to readjust and they would lose their night vision—which could be very dangerous in battle. So the soldiers were taught to cover one eye with their hand when a flash of light went off. That was all it took to preserve their night vision.

God has something He wants us to see in the darkness, but it is not enemy soldiers. The Lord says in Isaiah 45:3, "And I will give thee the treasures of darkness, and hidden riches of secret places, that thou mayest know that I, the LORD, which call thee by thy name, am the God of Israel." God has a storehouse of blessings for us to behold, but there are times when our greatest treasures are discovered in the darkness. Don't get the idea that darkness is always the work of the evil one. It is also one of God's ways to teach.

The stars that hang like chandeliers in the velvet canopy of space are only seen in the darkness. The stars do not come out at night. They are there all the time, and sometimes, on the darkest night, the stars seem the brightest.

The darkness may hide that which is near but reveal that which is far away. We may see more clearly in the daytime, but we see much farther at night. In the daylight we make think the brightest thoughts, but at night we think the deepest thoughts.

Does God have you in the darkness? Don't run away and seek your own light, but stay there with Him in the dark, and let the Holy Spirit develop your night vision so you can see the treasures God has for you in the darkness.

IT IS BETTER TO LEAN ON GOD IN THE DARKNESS THAN TO STAND ALONE IN MAN-MADE LIGHT

One of the greatest temptations we face when the darkness descends is to try and avoid it by generating our own light. Isaiah 50:11 contains a solemn warning about trying to light our own fire and drive the darkness away when God has other plans for us: "Behold, all ye that kindle a fire, that compass yourselves about with sparks: walk in the light of your fire, and in the sparks that ye have kindled. This shall ye have of mine hand; ye shall lie down in sorrow."

Anytime we try to blaze our own trail apart from God, we are headed for sorrow. We tend to forget that the darkness is ordained of God. "I [God] clothe the heavens with blackness, and I make sackcloth their covering" (Isaiah 50:3). We have nothing to fear from the darkness if we are there by God's sovereign purpose and loving will.

Remember that the darkness is merely the absence of light. The dark has never chased away the light. No one can open the door and let the darkness in. The night does not chase away the day, but it is the day that chases away the night. God is in control of both the light and the darkness, and He can chase away the darkness we experience with the smallest shaft of His light.

The Bible says that if we light our own fires and then try to walk in that light, we will ultimately lie down in sorrow. Abraham kindled his own fire when God's promise of a son and an heir did not materialize after the passage of time.

As far as Abraham was concerned, he was in the darkness, and he got tired of waiting on God. So he produced Ishmael (Genesis 16:1-16), who was not the son of promise. Much sorrow came into Abraham's heart because he could not wait on God. And today the children of Abraham in Israel are still lying down in sorrow because of their conflict with the descendants of Ishmael.

The same was true of Moses. He received a promise from God and was walking in the light, but then there was a time of darkness. Moses took things into his own hands and tried to liberate his people Israel from Egypt. He killed an Egyptian slave-master, and the one who started out to be a missionary became a murderer (Exodus 2:11-15). Moses' act set the work of God back forty years while Moses lived in the desert and made his way back into God's light at the burning bush.

Think of Simon Peter in the New Testament. He loved the Lord and boasted that he would follow Jesus to prison and to death (Luke 22:33). But then came dark Gethsemane, and Peter did not understand what was happening. He tried to light his own fire and ended up cutting off the ear of a servant to the high priest. What an embarrassment to the cause of Christ! It was a dark night for Peter, who should have waited on the Lord. Because Peter failed to do so, then even denied Christ, he would lie down in sorrow. The apostle wept bitterly that terrible night.

IF YOUR SUN HAS SET, BE SURE THAT MORNING WILL COME

Let me encourage you with the reminder that your dark night will come to an end. God will turn every hurt to a hallelujah and every tear to a pearl. Your Calvary will one day be an Easter. God's Word says, "The LORD God hath given me the tongue of the learned, that I should know how to speak a word in season to him that is weary: he wakeneth morning by morning, he wakeneth mine ear to hear as the learned" (Isaiah 50:4).

It was a dark night for the disciples when Jesus was nailed on the cross and hung there in three hours of literal darkness. Then there was the spiritual darkness surrounding His death and burial. It all seemed to be so inky black. His kingdom had shrunk to the narrow dimensions of a grave.

But then came that glorious morning of resurrection. The psalmist writes, "Unto the upright there ariseth light in the darkness: he is gracious, and full of compassion, and righteous" (Psalm 112:4). And again, "For his anger endureth but a moment; in his favour is life: weeping may endure for a night, but joy cometh in the morning" (Psalm 30:5).

Did not David say that he would walk *through* the valley of the shadow of death? The darkness will not swallow you up when you are there with the Lord. Remember that the God who leads you into the darkness is the God who will lead you through it. One day Jesus will pull back the shades of night and pin them with a star. He will open the door of the morning and flood your world with the sunshine of His love. And that day will be all the more wonderful after the darkness.

But the darkness is part of God's plan. Sometimes He has to take us into the dark to get the glare of the world out of our eyes so we can see clearly. We have this assurance from Scripture: "Yea, the darkness hideth not from thee; but the night shineth as the day: the darkness and the light are both alike to thee" (Psalm 139:12). God sees *through* the dark, and His eyes are upon you in your darkness.

I heard the story of a little girl whose mother died. Her first night apart from her mother was difficult. She felt alone in the darkness of her bedroom and left it to sleep with her father. They tried to get some sleep, but the little girl said, "Daddy, it is so dark. Have you ever seen it so dark?"

The father said, "No, darling, I have never seen it this dark."

Then the little girl, who could not even see her father's face in the dark, asked him, "Daddy, is your face toward me?"

"Yes, darling, my face is toward you."

"Daddy, you love me through the dark, don't you?"

"Yes, sweetheart, Daddy loves you through the dark."

With that assurance, the little girl drifted off to sleep.

Later that father slipped out of the bed, fell on his knees, and prayed, "Heavenly Father, it is so dark. Is Your face toward me?"

The answer came from heaven, "Yes, My child, My face is toward you."

"Heavenly Father, You love me through the dark, don't You?"

"Yes, My child, I love you through the darkest night."

And with that assurance, the father joined his precious daughter in much-needed sleep.

If the lights have gone out and you are in the dark, ask God to help you learn the lessons that can only be learned in darkness. And thank Him that He loves you through the dark and will one day flood you with His light once again.

5

Rejected Light

The Destiny of Those in Darkness

In today's world of political correctness, inclusiveness, extreme tolerance, and postmodern fogginess, an imposing question is often directed to the Bible-believing Christian: "Is Jesus Christ the only way to heaven, or is He just one of many religious teachers who show the way to heaven? Is He just one more selection on the smorgasbord of religious offerings for selective appetites?"

Often when I am interviewed by the secular media, I am asked a "gotcha" version of this same question in which the claims of Jesus to be the only way to heaven are used as an attempt to trap me. The question I am often asked goes something like this: "If you believe that your faith is the only true one, do you therefore believe that someone in the Jewish faith is lost?"

The purpose of this question is to put me between the proverbial "rock and a hard place." If I say yes, I appear bigoted and narrow. If I say no, I deny the exclusiveness of the gospel of Jesus.

My answer is, "I believe that one of my own children without Jesus Christ would be lost. It is not a matter of race or place, but of grace. No one is lost because he is a Jew or saved because he is a Gentile. Anyone who is saved, however, will be saved by the grace of God."

That, however, brings a more difficult question to the surface. Millions of people have died without ever hearing the name
of Jesus, and millions more are at risk of dying today without
ever hearing His name. How can we reconcile this inescapable fact
with the love and grace of God? Is our God righteous, fair, and just
in His dealings? If He is, how could He let a person die and go to
hell without ever once hearing the name of Jesus?

This question concerns many sincere believers, and unbelievers have used it as an excuse to keep from coming to the Lord
Jesus Christ. Some people would argue that if God is indeed fair
and just, there has to be another way to heaven other than believing in Jesus for people in this situation.

We are going to address the matter from God's Word in this
chapter, but let me state my thesis up front and then support it
from Scripture. *God is righteous and just in all of His ways,
and there is no other way to heaven apart from faith in Jesus
Christ.*

We must not succumb to the popular and sentimental idea
that the world's religions are all somehow connected and lead
to the same place. Jesus Christ said, "Verily, verily, I say unto you,
I am the door of the sheep. All that ever came before me are
thieves and robbers: but the sheep did not hear them" (John 10:7-
8). And in the Upper Room our Lord said, "I am the way, the
truth, and the life: no man cometh unto the Father, but by me"
(John 14:6).

Now if somebody can go to heaven some other way, that
makes Jesus a liar. And if Jesus Christ is a liar, then He cannot be
anybody's Savior because He cannot be trusted. If Jesus is not
the only way to heaven, then He is none of the ways.

God is righteous, and Jesus is the only way of salvation. But we still must ask how a righteous, good, and loving God can let a person who has never heard the name of Jesus die and go to hell. I am grateful we don't have to answer this question in our own wisdom, because the apostle Paul answered it for us in the first chapter of Romans.

GOD'S COURT IS CONVENED

Romans 1:18-23 is a very important section of Scripture, for in it Paul vindicates God's righteousness and shows Him to be absolutely just in holding every man accountable before Him— even those who have not had an opportunity to hear the gospel. Acting as the prosecutor in God's behalf, Paul states the indictment lodged in heaven's court: "For the wrath of God is revealed from heaven against all ungodliness and unrighteousness of men, who hold the truth in unrighteousness" (v. 18). In the verses that follow, the apostle will lay out the charges that prove the validity of this indictment.

Even the person who lives in the deepest spiritual darkness will be without excuse before God on the day of judgment, as hard as that may be for some of us to understand. I want to give you four factors from Romans 1 that, when taken together, will help you understand this matter of the destiny of those in darkness.

THE REVELATION FACTOR: ALL MEN HAVE SOME LIGHT

The first factor I want you to see is the revelation factor, which is that *all people have received some light from God*. The Bible says that every person is the beneficiary of two powerful witnesses to the existence and nature of God. Let's imagine the scene in heaven at the time we know as the final judgment. Those who have never heard the gospel of Jesus Christ hear the indictment read that they are without excuse before God and under sentence of His eternal wrath because of their ungodliness and unrighteousness.

But they enter this plea: "Your Honor, we never heard the gospel. We never knew how to be saved. We are innocent by reason of ignorance."

In answer, Paul, the prosecuting attorney, presents his two witnesses that testify of God's reality. God is just to hold all men accountable "because that which may be known of God is manifest in them; for God hath showed it unto them. For the invisible things of him from the creation of the world are clearly seen, being understood by the things that are made, even his eternal power and Godhead; so that they are without excuse" (vv. 19-20).

These two witnesses are the external witness of *creation* and the internal witness of *conscience*. No one can say he has never had a chance to know about God because God has revealed Himself in creation and in the human heart.

Creation Witnesses to the Power of God

Creation testifies to God's existence. "The heavens declare the glory of God; and the firmament showeth his handiwork" (Psalm 19:1). Creation demands a Creator, and God's Word says the Creator is known by His creation. When I see an intricately made watch, I have to say that someone crafted it. When I see a building that displays symmetry and balance and purpose, I know there is an architect behind it. And when I see this mighty universe, I realize that it took superior intelligence to put it all together.

The testimony of creation all around us is powerful and undeniable, because it is outward and objective. The very scientists and other experts who deny the existence of God are the ones telling us how intricate our world is. To see the creation and deny the Creator is foolishness. The only alternative to faith is to believe that nothing times nobody equals everything. That is inexcusable foolishness.

Conscience Witnesses to the Presence of God

But there is a second witness that no one can escape, which is the internal, subjective witness of the human conscience. This is what Paul referred to when he wrote, "That which may be known of God is manifest in them" (Romans 1:19). We read further of this witness in Romans 2:14-15:

> *For when the Gentiles, which have not the law, do by nature the things contained in the law, these, having not the law, are a law unto themselves: which show the work of the law written in their hearts, their conscience also bearing witness, and their thoughts the mean while accusing or else excusing one another.*

The word "Gentiles" here is another word for pagans, people who have never heard the gospel. Even these people know the basic requirements of God's holy law because these things are written on their hearts. So even if we are talking about the most primitive culture on earth, its inhabitants know in their hearts that it is wrong to kill another person. They know it is wrong to steal and lie, because when they do they are smitten in their consciences.

The human conscience is one reason missionaries can go to pagan societies with the gospel and find a hearing. Without this internal knowledge of God, they would have little to appeal to as they present the gospel. But the gospel hits home because its message agrees with the witness of the heart that there is guilt before God that needs to be dealt with.

Pagans also have a built-in knowledge of God. Augustine said the soul of man is restless until it rests in God. God made us to know and serve Him, and until we do we are like round pegs in square holes. There has never been a society on earth in which the people do not have some sense of a God to be feared, worshiped, and appeased.

Back in the 1920s a famous anthropologist claimed to have found a culture in the Pacific that had no God-consciousness whatever. Her reports were widely touted as proving that human beings had no innate knowledge of God, which was viewed as something imposed from without. But years after this anthropologist's death, evidence came out that she had doctored her reports, and her conclusions were called into question.

The fact is that there is no such thing as a true intellectual atheist, someone who says he simply cannot believe in God for lack of evidence. People who claim to be atheists do so not because of intellectual problems, but because of moral problems. The Bible does not say, "The intellectual has said in his mind, 'There is no God.'" What does the Scripture say? "The fool hath said *in his heart*, There is no God" (Psalm 53:1, emphasis added).

Belief in God is not a matter of intelligence, but of morality.

An atheist is somebody whose inborn knowledge of God makes him uncomfortable. So he tells himself that if he can get rid of the idea of God, he can get rid of his uncomfortable feeling. But that does not work for him. He is like the man who bought a new boomerang and almost killed himself trying to throw the old one away.

An atheist can never completely get rid of the knowledge that there is a God to whom he is accountable. Neither can a pagan who has never heard the name of Christ. Make no mistake: *All men have some light from God and are accountable for that light.* John said of Jesus Christ, "That was the true Light, which lighteth every man that cometh into the world" (John 1:9). The revelation factor says that God has given all people the witness of creation and conscience.

In his book *The Emmanuel Factor* Nelson Price tells of a friend who owns a large trucking company. "His company has offices in approximately 150 cities across America. In considering a person for employment a polygraph test is given. The operator of the 'lie-detecting' device has provided [my friend] with a sworn affidavit regarding one part of the test given to every would-be employee. The operator asks, 'Do you believe there is a God?' In every instance when a professing atheist answered, 'No,' the test has shown the person to be lying" (Broadman Press, 1987, p. 15).

THE REFUSAL FACTOR: LIGHT REFUSED INCREASES DARKNESS

The second factor that helps us understand the destiny of those in darkness is the refusal factor, which says that *light refused increases darkness.*

Going back to Romans 1, Paul continues his indictment in the courtroom of God. Those who do not know Christ are without excuse, "Because that, when they knew God, they glorified him not as God, neither were thankful; but became vain in their imaginations, and their foolish heart was *darkened*" (v. 21, italics added). People are justly condemned who turn their backs on the light that creation and conscience afford them.

No one can take God's light or truth and simply store it away. When God gives a person light, even if it is the more limited light of creation and conscience, if that person does not turn toward the light and seek to know and glorify God, he does not remain static but begins to regress and loses even the light that he has. His foolish heart will be darkened.

The Opposite of Truth Is Sin

Here's an important principle I don't want you to miss. In the Bible the opposite of truth is not error, but sin. Now there may indeed be error involved, but that error is the baggage that comes with the sin. This antithesis between truth and sin is evident in Romans 1:18, where the word "hold" means to suppress the truth or push it down.

The man who refuses the truth shoves it back down into the deepest recesses of his soul and tries to smother it. He does this not in error because he misunderstands the truth, but in sin because he does not want to submit to the truth. He realizes that to believe in God means he has to adjust his lifestyle. A person in this condition turns away from the light and toward the darkness, and because of his foolish decision his heart is darkened.

The Delusion of the Lost

We see this graphically demonstrated in 2 Thessalonians 2:8-12, which I think are some of the most terrifying verses in the Bible because they speak of the coming of the Antichrist and the terrible delusion that will come on the world of unbelievers:

> *And then shall that Wicked be revealed. . . . Even him, whose coming is after the working of Satan with all power and signs and lying wonders, and with all deceivableness of unrighteousness in them that perish; because they received not the love of the truth, that they might be saved. And for this cause God shall send them strong delusion, that they should believe a lie: That they all might be damned who believed not the truth, but had pleasure in unrighteousness.*

Does it shock you to think that God would send people a delusion to cause them to believe a lie? That's what the Word of God says. And it gets even stronger, for the reason God sends them a delusion is so that they might be eternally condemned.

Why would God do this? What kind of people invite such harsh judgment? Look at the text again. They did not love and believe the truth but found their pleasure in unrighteousness. They knew the truth but turned from it because they loved their sin! Their problem is not intellectual but moral.

Perhaps I can illustrate it this way. Let's say that a man comes to our church in Memphis for the first time. He happens to come on a Sunday when we are emphasizing the need for salvation and the doom of the lost; so he hears a message about the reality of hell and the need to receive Christ.

But because this man is extremely prideful and doesn't want to admit that he has a spiritual need, he leaves church highly insulted and steaming mad. "I'm never going back there again. How dare that preacher tell me I'm condemned!"

Now let's suppose that later on this man is sitting at home one Sunday watching television when the doorbell rings. He answers it to find two members from a false cult standing there. They start talking and assure this man that there is no hell. He invites them in and begins to believe the lie that there is no hell, even though he is lost and condemned and on the road to the very hell he says he doesn't believe in. Like many in the cults, he may be sincere, but he is sincerely wrong.

What is this man's problem? It's not that he has carefully studied what the Bible says about hell and concluded that the Word is in error. His problem is that he loves his pride and his sin and doesn't want to admit that what the Bible says about him is true. So he refuses God's light and hooks up with this false religion, and he is led deeper into darkness.

Jesus said, "If thine eye be evil, thy whole body shall be full of darkness. If therefore the light that is in thee be darkness, how great is that darkness!" (Matthew 6:23). Light refused brings darkness—and the sad thing is that many people who are in darkness think they are in the light. "Professing themselves to be wise, they became fools" (Romans 1:22). People may have Ph.D. degrees, but if they reject the truth of Christ, their degree translates to "Phenomenal Dud."

THE RECEPTION FACTOR: LIGHT OBEYED INCREASES LIGHT

The refusal factor is a hard truth to consider because it confronts us with the fact that people willfully reject God's light.

But there is also the reception factor, which says that *light obeyed increases light*.

It is important that you understand this because you may be saying at this point, "There is a problem here. You said that no one can go to heaven apart from Jesus Christ, but you also said that the light of creation and conscience is not enough by itself to bring salvation. You said that people need to trust in Jesus."

This is absolutely right. The light that men receive from creation around them and their conscience within is not enough to save them. It is, however, enough to condemn them, because a person who is not interested in the reality of God is certainly not going to be interested in the way to God. And God is under no obligation to give any further revelation to a man who becomes vain in his imagination and darkens his foolish heart.

The Importance of Faith

But the question we're considering now is, what about the person who has never heard of Jesus but responds to the light he has? To answer this I want to go back a few verses to Romans 1:16-17, one of the greatest statements about the gospel ever made. "For I am not ashamed of the gospel of Christ: for it is the power of God unto salvation to every one that believeth; to the Jew first, and also to the Greek. For therein is the righteousness of God revealed from faith to faith: as it is written, The just shall live by faith."

The phrase I want to focus on is this: "The righteousness of God [is] revealed from faith to faith." The wonderful thing about our great God is that when we come to the light that He gives us, He gives us more light! When we believe God, He reveals more of His truth to us. Jesus said, "Take heed therefore how ye hear:

for whosoever hath, to him shall be given" (Luke 8:18). The more you obey the light, the more light you will be given. This is the reception factor—"from faith to faith."

How does this apply to those who have never heard the name of Jesus? Here's a man living in spiritual darkness, perhaps in the deepest recesses of the Amazon jungle. God speaks to him through creation and his conscience, and he says, "God, I believe that You exist, and I want to know You."

That is an expression of faith, no matter how primitive, and if this man continues walking toward the light he has, he will go from faith to faith until he comes to the Lord Jesus Christ. God will give him more light as he receives and responds to the light he has. When a person's heart is open to receive the gospel, God will get the gospel to that person if He has to parachute a missionary into the jungle.

God Will Respond to Honest Seekers

The reception factor teaches that God will not leave in darkness people who are seeking Him. I believe with all of my heart there's never been a man or woman on the face of this earth who honestly lived up to the light God gave them and yet died without an opportunity to receive Christ. God is too righteous and loving to leave honest seekers in the dark.

We can see illustrations of this in history. Missionaries have reported taking the gospel to primitive peoples who have never heard of Christ and finding the soil of their hearts prepared through creation and conscience. One tribe told the missionaries who came with the good news of Christ, "We've been worshiping Him. We just didn't know His name until now."

We also see illustrations of the reception factor in the Bible.

The experience of the Ethiopian eunuch (Acts 8:26-40) is similar to that of this modern-day tribe. This official was heading home to north Africa in his chariot after going all the way to Jerusalem to seek and worship the true God.

But this man's heart was still disturbed as he rode along, because even though he had been to the most religious city on earth, the wells of religion were dry. And so he was perplexed as he sat reading from Isaiah 53 and trying to understand of whom the prophet was speaking (Acts 8:30-32). The eunuch was living up to the light he had by seeking God. So what did God do? He sent an angel to Samaria to summon a preacher named Philip, who was in the middle of a big revival campaign.

The angel told Philip, "Arise, and go toward the south unto the way that goeth down from Jerusalem unto Gaza, which is desert" (Acts 8:26). Philip obeyed and went and found one solitary man who needed someone to tell him how to be saved.

There was another man in the book of Acts, a Roman centurion named Cornelius, who was a Gentile worshiper of the God of Israel (Acts 10:1-2). Cornelius had a hunger to know God. I don't know where he got that hunger. Perhaps he looked up into the starry heavens one night and said to himself, "This could not have just happened. There must be a God somewhere." Maybe Cornelius had prayed, "O God, whoever You are, wherever You are, whatever You are, I want to know You."

The Bible says that Cornelius prayed to God continually, and God honored his hunger by giving him a vision in which he was instructed to send for Simon Peter in Joppa (vv. 3-6). Cornelius sent two messengers to Peter, and as they were on their way Peter was given his own vision (vv. 10-16). As he puzzled over its meaning, the Holy Spirit assured Peter that God wanted him to go speak to Cornelius (vv. 19-20). The result was that Cornelius and his entire household got saved. Cornelius obeyed the light he had, and God gave him the saving light of the gospel.

The Problem Is in the Heart

You see, the real issue that unbelievers need to face is not the amount of light they have, but what they do with the light they have. In other words, the problem is not in the head but in the heart.

One of the greatest promises in the Bible is John 7:17. The people of Israel were wondering about Jesus, and the Pharisees were testing and taunting Him. So Jesus said to them, "My doctrine is not mine, but his that sent me. If any man will do his will, he shall know of the doctrine, whether it be of God, or whether I speak of myself" (vv. 16b-17).

Anyone who wants to know whether Jesus Christ is a deceiving liar, a deluded lunatic, or the divine Lord of all only has to be willing to do God's will, and the truth will be revealed.

One of the most dramatic examples of this principle at work in my own ministry happened many years ago when I was pastoring a church in Merritt Island, Florida, at the time that man first went to the moon, when Neil Armstrong and his crew were sent into space. The incident is still vivid in my mind and heart and wonderfully illustrates what God does when a person decides to obey the light he has.

I was in my office one day when a man drove up in a big Cadillac, parked it in front of the church, and came in to see me. He was an important member of the space program at Cape Canaveral that was trying to put a man on the moon.

He began by saying, "I need to talk to you about my wife.

She wants to commit suicide, and I don't want her to. Will you talk to her?"

I replied, "I'll talk to her if you'll come with her." He agreed, and soon the two of them were sitting in my office. I asked the woman to tell me about her problem, which turned out to be the man sitting beside her! This poor woman's husband was a liar, drunkard, adulterer, gambler, blasphemer, and abuser.

So I stopped talking to his wife and said to this highly placed man in the space industry, "Sir, are you a Christian?" I wasn't asking for information but just trying to get the conversation started.

He laughed scornfully and said, "No, I'm not a Christian! I'm an atheist."

"Oh, I see," I replied. "An atheist is someone who says he knows beyond any doubt that there is no God. Let me ask you something. Would you say that you know half of everything there is to know?"

"Oh no, of course not."

"But you said you know there is no God. Wouldn't you have to admit the possibility that God might exist in that part of the universe's knowledge that you don't have?"

"OK," he said. "You got me. I'm not an atheist—I'm an agnostic." I didn't tell him that the Latin equivalent of the word *agnostic* is *ignoramus* (literally, "we are ignorant of"). It means the same thing in Greek or Latin. A person who calls himself an agnostic is saying he's just plain ignorant.

"Well," I replied, "an agnostic is just a fancy word for a doubter. Are you a doubter?"

"Yes, I'm a doubter, and a big one."

I said, "I don't care what size of doubter you are, but what kind." He asked me to explain. So I pointed out that there are honest and dishonest doubters. He wanted to know the difference. So I told him that an honest doubter doesn't know, but he wants to know and therefore he investigates. But a dishonest doubter doesn't know because he doesn't want to know, and he can't find God for the same reason a thief can't find a police officer. I showed this man the challenge from Jesus Christ in John 7:17 that says, in effect, that anyone who really wants to know the truth can know.

That got him to thinking. So I made him this offer. "Would you like to find out whether you're an honest or dishonest doubter?" He said he would. So I asked him if he would sign a statement that read something like this: "God, I don't know whether You exist or whether the Bible is Your Word. I don't know whether Jesus Christ is Your Son. But I want to know. So I will make an honest investigation and follow the results wherever they lead me, regardless of the outcome or cost."

He wasn't sure he wanted to sign the statement and asked me to give it to him again. I read it again, and he agreed to follow it. I told him that was wonderful and gave him an assignment. "I want you to begin reading the Gospel of John, because it was written that you might believe Jesus is the Christ and by believing have eternal life in His name."

"But I don't believe," he objected.

"That's all right. Just make an honest investigation into the facts. Say to God, 'I don't know if this is Your Word, but if it is, then show me, and I will obey You if You will speak to my heart.'" He agreed that was fair enough and went out.

In a few weeks he came back to my office and said, "I believe

Jesus Christ is the Son of God." He got on his knees and, like a little child, wept his way into the arms of Jesus.

The change was immediate. Later that week I saw this man and his wife sitting in their Cadillac, holding hands like school kids. That all took place many years ago. Recently I got a letter from this man telling me of his joy in the Lord. In that letter he said, "I want to thank you for spending time with this general in the devil's army."

This man thought his problems were intellectual, but they were moral. When he surrendered his will to God and followed the light, God flooded him with more light until he was standing in the full blaze of Calvary. Light obeyed brings more light.

THE RECKONING FACTOR: MEN ARE JUDGED ACCORDING TO THE LIGHT THEY HAVE REJECTED

The fourth and final factor I want to discuss is the reckoning factor. When unbelievers stand before God, He is not going to judge them by the sins they have committed, but by *the light they have rejected*. This is very clear in the Word of God. Speaking of the righteousness of God, Paul writes, "But after thy hardness and impenitent heart treasurest up unto thyself wrath against the day of wrath and revelation of the righteous judgment of God . . ." (Romans 2:5). Then in verses 11-12 the apostle says, "For there is no respect of persons with God. For as many as have sinned without law shall also perish without law: and as many as have sinned in the law shall be judged by the law."

Paul is saying that God knows how much light each person has, and He is going to judge people by the light they have rejected. This is why the Bible can say, ". . . that every mouth may be stopped, and all the world may become guilty before God"

(Romans 3:19). We in this country have far more light than most people in the world, not necessarily because we sought it, but because we received it by the kindness and providence of God. But He is also going to hold us more accountable than the person who has never heard the gospel.

Jesus emphasized this when He contrasted God's judgment upon people who knew better and those we would call pagans who lived in ignorance: "That servant, which knew his lord's will, and prepared not himself, neither did according to his will, shall be beaten with many stripes. But he that knew not, and did commit things worthy of stripes, shall be beaten with few stripes. For unto whomsoever much is given, of him shall be much required: and to whom men have committed much, of him will they ask the more" (Luke 12:47-48).

It would be bad enough for a person to die and go to hell who had never heard the name of Jesus and refused to live up to the light that he did have. But how much worse it will be for a person who has all the advantages we enjoy and yet rejects Christ.

Jesus said to Capernaum, the city that served as His head-quarters during His earthly ministry, "And thou, Capernaum, which art exalted unto heaven, shalt be brought down to hell: for if the mighty works, which have been done in thee, had been done in Sodom, it would have remained until this day. But I say unto you, That it shall be more tolerable for the land of Sodom in the day of judgment, than for thee" (Matthew 11:23-24). Jesus preached, taught, and performed miracles in Capernaum; yet the people turned their backs on Him and never received Him.

In the end, the burning question is not what God is going to do with those who have never heard. We can trust God to be completely righteous and just in His dealings with them. The burning question is whether you and I who know the truth have responded to the light we have been given by coming to the Lord Jesus Christ for salvation.

I pray that you know the Lord as your Savior, dear reader. If there is any doubt in your mind, please close this book, and don't do anything else until you settle the issue of your soul's eternal destiny. I promise you on the authority of God's Word that if you will believe in Jesus, He will save you. The Bible says, "As many as received him [Jesus], to them gave he power to become the sons of God, even to them that believe on his name" (John 1:12).

6

Enjoying the Light

Making Every Day a Great Day

A man was drinking coffee, reading the newspaper, and paying no attention to his wife at breakfast one morning. She leaned over and pulled the paper down, looked into his face, and said, "I bet you don't even remember what today is."

Panic flew through the man as he thought for a moment and quickly tried to cover himself. "Of course, I do! Do you think I could ever forget?"

That day at noon his wife received a dozen red roses. Later in the day a gorgeous black negligee arrived, followed still later by a large box of chocolates. When the husband came home that evening, there was soft candlelight glowing throughout the house. The table was beautifully set with a white linen tablecloth and fresh-cut flowers. Soft music was playing, and his wife was dressed to the nines. They had a romantic meal.

Afterward she came over, gave her husband a wonderful kiss, and said, "Sweetheart, I want to thank you for making this the most wonderful Groundhog Day I've ever had."

I guess some of us are better than others at remembering special days. But there is a day that all of us need to remember as special, and that day is today. I want you to know that it is possible for you to live 365 days a year without having a bad day if you learn how to stand in the light of God.

The Bible says of today, "This is the day which the LORD hath made; we will rejoice and be glad in it" (Psalm 118:24). Here are five biblical facts about this day and every day that will help you make it special—for when we make every God-given day a God-governed day, it will be a God-gladdened day.

Psalm 118:24 has a prophetic application because it is part of a passage that looks forward to that glorious day when Jesus Christ will bring salvation. But this wonderful verse also has a practical application for each day in the week. Let me show you how to make every day a great day as you enjoy God's light.

TODAY IS A PROVIDED DAY

The psalmist declares that this is a day God has made. Would it surprise you to learn that the word "made" in Psalm 118:24 is the same word used throughout Genesis 1—2 for God's work in creation? God created this universe with meticulous attention to detail, and the Bible says that He uses the same care in fashioning each day.

One of God's creations and gifts to us is the gift of time. In every day there is time to work, serve, love, and laugh. But like any gift, the value we receive from the time allotted to us is up to us. Today is a gift we have from God, and because it is God's gift we are stewards of it.

When we stand before Jesus Christ, we will give an account for this day and every day that we live. There are twenty-four hours, 1,440 minutes, 86,400 seconds in every day. All people have the same amount of time each day. The only difference is how they use the time given to them.

I read about a man who had a seven-million-dollar watch built for him by Swiss watchmakers. I can hardly imagine how much gold, silver, precious stones, and intricate workmanship it would take to make a watch worth seven million dollars. But I laughed as I read the story, because I thought to myself, the man who is wearing this fabulously expensive watch has no more time than someone wearing a twenty-dollar watch from the corner drugstore.

Time is one of the very few areas of life where we are all on equal footing, the great and the small alike. The Lord has made and given you this day for your use and blessing and His glory. How would you spend these twenty-four hours if you knew Jesus was coming back tomorrow? Then get at it!

TODAY IS A PRESENT DAY

"This *is* the day which the LORD hath made," says the Scripture (emphasis added). Notice the present tense of this verb. The psalmist is not looking back to the past or ahead to the future, but his focus is on the present day before us. If God thinks that today is special enough to merit His creative attention, He must have something special in it for us.

Don't Let Yesterday Steal Today from You

But keeping our focus on the "presentness" of today is not always easy. There are two days that can steal the strength and joy from today. Today is often crucified between these two thieves known as yesterday and tomorrow. Yesterday can be the enemy of today if we insist on living in the past. But why would people dwell on yesterday?

One reason is *past guilt*. Some people are haunted by the ghost of guilt for things that have happened. A man told his pastor he had done a terrible thing and could find no rest in his conscience. The pastor asked him, "Have you confessed it to the Lord?"

The man replied, "Pastor, I've confessed that sin a thousand times."

The wise pastor said, "That is 999 times too many. You should confess it once and praise God a thousand times for His forgiveness."

Another reason some people live in the past is because they are trying to recapture *past glory*. Many professional athletes struggle to get their lives together after retirement because they have a hard time facing the fact that they are no longer in the spotlight. One former Major League pitcher said, "All this time you think you're gripping the ball, and it turns out that the ball was gripping you."

Athletes aren't the only ones who long for past glory. I'm afraid you can go to many churches today where not much is happening for the kingdom of God. If you were to ask a church member about it, he might say, "Yes, but you should have seen this place thirty years ago when Pastor So-and-So was here. Those were great days!"

My friend, are you still trying to bask in the light of faded glory from yesterday? Today would be a great day to step out of those shadows and stand in the new light God has for you today.

Paul was the greatest missionary, apostle, and church builder who ever lived, but he refused to live off past glory. His determination was clear: "I count not myself to have apprehended: but this one thing I do, forgetting those things which are behind, and reaching forth unto those things which are before, I press toward the mark for the prize of the high calling of God in Christ Jesus" (Philippians 3:13-14).

Many of the things we have done may be great and wonderful, but they are yesterday's victories. My former football coach used to tell us before we played, "Boys, put away those press clippings. The other team hasn't read them."

A third thing that keeps some people tied to the past is *past grief*. Have you known problems and sorrow? Are there heartaches you have endured? These things are real, but you don't need to deny their reality to make up your mind that you are going to stop licking your wounds and feeling sorry for yourself. Past grief will not heal your heart but will only tie you to yesterday.

Past grudges are yet another reason some people cannot enjoy the today that God gives them. Have you been mistreated? I have never met anyone who hasn't been wronged somewhere along the way. Don't drag a heavy load of resentment from yesterday into today. Resentment and grudges only weigh down the person carrying them. There is no quicker way to poison today than to infect it with the bitter gall from a past hurt.

Tomorrow Is Also a Thief of Today

Other people fail to enjoy today because they are living in anticipation or dread of tomorrow. I read of a psychologist who asked three thousand people this question: "What do you have to live for?" He reported that 94 percent of the people said they were enduring today while anticipating tomorrow.

The sad thing is that while people like this are waiting for tomorrow, they are missing today. There's nothing wrong with having hope and optimism about the future. But if your hopes for what might happen tomorrow make today seem like a drudgery to be endured, you will never fully understand what it means to rejoice and be glad in today.

The problem is that many people's hopes for tomorrow are based not on God's presence and promises, but on wishful thinking or even foolish dreams. Millions of people in this country play the lottery every day because, they think, tomorrow may be the day they get lucky and hit it big.

Almost all of our state governments sponsor and vigorously promote this cruel game of "no chance" that separates the weak and greedy from money they can't afford to lose. The Illinois lottery commission once ran a television advertisement in which a young man is sitting in his office cubicle when a friend comes by and says, "Hey, your lucky numbers finally won today!"

But instead of rejoicing, the man lowers his head and begins banging it on his file cabinet. Then he raises his face to the camera and with a pained look says, "I forgot to play."

The punch line of the ad was, "You can't win if you don't play." The message was obvious: Don't forget to buy your lottery ticket or you might miss out tomorrow.

Some people are waiting for tomorrow in anticipation. But there are others who are worrying about tomorrow in dread. Our Lord has warned against this. "Take therefore no thought for the morrow: for the morrow shall take thought for the things of itself. Sufficient unto the day is the evil thereof" (Matthew 6:34).

The context of this famous verse is worry over whether we will have enough to eat or drink or wear tomorrow (read vv. 25-33). Jesus told us not to worry about tomorrow because God knows our needs and will provide.

But there is another good reason for not worrying about tomorrow. God has a very delicate ecology for the soul. He allows enough difficulty in every day to cause us to come to Him and lean upon Him, and then gives us enough strength to meet the difficulty.

God allows the difficulty so that we might see our need of Him, but He gives the strength so that we might be blessed by Him. However, God only gives today's strength for today's needs. "As thy days, so shall thy strength be" is the promise of God's Word (Deuteronomy 33:25).

Worry Is a Waste of Time and Life

Think about it. Worry does not take the sorrow out of tomorrow—it only takes the strength out of today. Why is this? Because today is the only day we have in which to worry.

A man was trying to encourage his friend not to be such a worrywart. "Worry is a waste of time," he said. "After all, 80 percent of the things people worry about never happen anyway."

"Aha!" the worrier cried. "That proves that worry works!" No, it doesn't prove any such thing. As Christians, we are *commanded* not to worry. God meets us today with today's grace and strength. Worry, therefore, does not make us ready for tomorrow but unready. We will face the future out of breath because we have been fighting tomorrow's battles today without the strength today for tomorrow's battles.

Worry pulls tomorrow's clouds over today's sunshine. I heard of a man who was constantly failing. He was a salesman who could hardly sell anything. He drove a shabby old car, his wife had a haggard, worried look, his kids were making poor grades, and he lived on the "wrong side of the tracks."

Then something happened to this man. He began to smile, stand up straight, and have a positive attitude. Before long he was driving a shiny new car, his wife had fixed herself up and was beautiful, his kids began to make good grades, and he moved his family into a new home.

His friend asked him, "What happened to you? I have never seen such a transformation!"

"Do you remember how I used to worry about everything? Well, I don't worry anymore."

"How did you do that?"

"I found a firm of professional worriers. I just go down at the beginning of each day and tell them my problems, and they do all my worrying for me while I go out and do my work. It really frees me up to be a good salesman."

His friend said, "Does it work?"

"Of course, it works," the man answered. "Look at the change it has made in me."

"But how much does it cost?" the friend wanted to know.

"One thousand dollars a week," came back the answer.

His friend gasped. "My goodness! How are you going to pay that much?"

The man smiled and said, "That's their worry!"

Wouldn't it be wonderful if there were someone who could carry our burdens for us so we don't have to worry? My friend, there is! His name is Jesus, but you don't have to pay Him a thousand dollars a week. His invitation to worry-free living is free: "Come unto me, all ye that labour and are heavy laden, and I will give you rest" (Matthew 11:28).

Peter, who accepted this wonderful invitation himself, tells us to cast all of our cares upon Jesus (1 Peter 5:7).

Yesterday is but a canceled check. Tomorrow is a promissory note. Today is all the cash we have, and we need to learn to spend it well. Someone has said, "Yesterday is history. Tomorrow is mystery. Today is a gift from God. That's why we call it the present."

TODAY IS A PRECIOUS DAY

Since God made today, it is precious, and we need to value today and every day as something precious. We are eternal beings, created by and for the eternal God. This makes time more than just a fleeting commodity. Because of who we are, there is something of eternity in every minute we live.

Time is life; so to waste time is to waste life. To kill time is suicide by degrees. The Bible urges us to take careful account of the minutes we have been given today. "See then that ye walk circumspectly, not as fools, but as wise, redeeming the time, because the days are evil" (Ephesians 5:15-16).

The art of living is to spend time wisely. Moses wrote, "So teach us to number our days, that we may apply our hearts unto wisdom" (Psalm 90:12). But how can we spend time wisely? Here are four ideas worth putting into practice.

1. Spend enough time with God to get a clear sense of His direction. It is never a waste of time to wait on God. There is enough time in every day to do all that God wants you to do. Jesus said, "I have finished the work which thou gavest me to do" (John 17:4).

If you want a prayer to guide you in seeking God's will each day, use this petition from Scripture: "LORD, lift thou up the light of thy countenance upon us" (Psalm 4:6). As we learned in the previous chapter, when we walk in the light we have, God floods our path with greater light. "In thy light shall we see light" (Psalm 36:9).

2. Set God-honoring priorities. Life is not always a simple choice between good and bad, but between the good and the best. Don't let the good steal the best from your day. I like the fact that Paul said, "This one thing I do" (Philippians 3:13), not "These twelve things I dabble in."

Perhaps the saddest thing in today's world is misplaced priorities. A woman said to her husband as he was leaving for work one day, "Sweetheart, don't forget that we are moving today. Don't come back to the old address."

"You don't need to remind me," he answered a little testily as he drove away. "Don't you think I can remember that?"

But sure enough, this man was so absorbed in his work that he drove back to the same house that evening. But this time the door was open, the paper was in the yard, and the house was empty of furniture.

He said to himself, "Oh, no! She said I would forget, and I did. To make matters worse, I don't remember where we've moved." Just then he saw a little boy on a bicycle and said, "Do you know the family that used to live here?"

"Yes, sir."

"Would you happen to know where they have moved?"

The little boy looked at him and said, "Daddy, Mama said you would forget." I submit that this was a man with misplaced priorities. We ought to say no to at least one thing each day so we can say yes to something more important.

3. Work in the power of the Holy Spirit. The Bible tells us to redeem the time, and in the same paragraph it commands us to be filled with the Spirit (Ephesians 5:16-18). How we work is as important as what we work on. For Christians, there are only two ways to operate: in the energy of the flesh or the power of the Spirit.

If you try to work in your own strength, you will wind up burning the wick and not the oil. Every day that is not a Spirit-filled day is a wasted day, for Jesus said, "Without me ye can do nothing" (John 15:5). Begin each day by asking the Holy Spirit of God to fill you, and thank Him for answering your prayer. Then draw on the Spirit for energy and power to maximize today.

4. *Recognize procrastination as a sin.* There are a lot of jokes about procrastination, but there's nothing funny about delayed obedience—which is really disobedience. The Bible has a strong word for the procrastinator: "To him that knoweth to do good, and doeth it not, to him it is a sin" (James 4:17).

We usually think of procrastination as putting off a chore like sweeping the garage or taking out the trash. Doing our work promptly is important, but more important is avoiding the mind-set that procrastination produces. This mind-set says we are going to begin laying aside that bad habit or developing that needed spiritual discipline . . . tomorrow.

Not so. We must learn the habit of immediate obedience. Today is too precious to put off its joys and tasks until tomorrow. This old piece of advice will stand you in good stead: If you want to develop character, do something you don't feel like doing when you don't feel like doing it.

TODAY IS A PASSING DAY

Today will soon be gone. The Lord Jesus realized this when He said, "I must work the works of him that sent me, while it is day: the night cometh, when no man can work" (John 9:4).

Time is a strange commodity. You can't save it, borrow it, loan it, leave it, or take it. There are only two things you can do with time: use it or lose it. Consider these truths about time:

Time can't be stopped. You can call time-out in a ball game, but not in life.

Time can't be stored. You can put money away in the bank, but not time.

Time can't be stretched. You can put another cup of water in the soup, but you cannot add a second to time.

Time can't be shared. I can give you many things, but I can't give you any of my time in the sense of taking hours from my life and adding them to yours. All I can do is spend time with you. Daylight Saving Time doesn't change anything except our clocks.

Given the passing nature of time, how important it is that we realize we must use today wisely. The pioneer missionary Robert Moffat said, "We shall have all eternity in which to celebrate our victories, but only one short hour before the sun sets in which to win them."

A woman once wrote to the late advice columnist Ann Landers, "I am thirty-six years old. They are trying to get me to go back and finish my education. But if I do that, I will be forty years old when I graduate. What do you think?"

I thought Ann Landers's answer was classic: "How old will you be four years from now if you do not go to college?"

The point is clear. Time is passing. Seize it while you can. Today is the most important day of your life.

Many times we think that we were near death after some accident or illness. But in reality we were not near death because we didn't die. Actually you are nearer death this moment than you have ever been.

Bob was a good friend of mine. He and I commuted to seminary together. He was handsome, tall, and sun-crowned—the specimen of a man.

One day Bob said to me, "Adrian, there is an old man who is very ill. He has had a serious heart attack, and I believe he only has days to live. Would you go by and speak to him about his relationship with the Lord?"

I said, "Of course, I will, Bob."

And I did. I went by and shared the gospel with this dear old man, and he prayed and asked Christ to come into his heart.

But that's not the end of the story. A few days later Bob was having lunch with his wife. They finished their meal, and Bob laid down his napkin and began to walk across the room. He gave a gasp, fell to the floor, and died suddenly of a heart attack.

The irony of it all is this. Bob said the old man had only a few days to live, but the man lived for years. It was Bob who had only a few days to live. No wonder the Bible teaches us to number our days that we might be wise, as we saw above in Psalm 90:12.

Now the thought that our days are limited need not be morbid. It can be a spur and an encouragement to make the most of each day. You've heard the old saying, "Today is the first day of the rest of your life." But the truth of the matter is that today may be the last day of the first part of your life. Your times are in God's hands, and you will be here as long as He has something for you to do. So rejoice and be glad in this wonderful day, and use it wisely.

TODAY IS A PROVIDENTIAL DAY

Psalm 118:24 concludes that since today is God's handicraft, "We will rejoice and be glad in it."

The secret of joy, therefore, is to see the providence of God in everything and rejoice in it. Nothing comes to you each day but what God somehow either arranges or allows. This is why Paul can write, "In every thing give thanks: for this is the will of God in Christ Jesus concerning you" (1 Thessalonians 5:18).

Again the great apostle exhorts us, "Be careful [anxious] for nothing; but in every thing by prayer and supplication with thanksgiving let your requests be made known unto God. And the peace of God, which passeth all understanding, shall keep your hearts and minds through Christ Jesus" (Philippians 4:6-7).

Read on a few more verses, and you will discover why Paul was able to rejoice in all circumstances. He told the Philippians, "I have learned, in whatsoever state I am, therewith to be content" (v. 11).

These Scriptures and many others remind us of the providence of God that is always at work in our lives and our need to respond with rejoicing. To rejoice is a choice.

A wonderful children's story tells of a gruff old man who hears a robin singing on his windowsill one winter day. The man is irritated by the robin's song and opens the window to ask the little bird why he is singing. The robin replies that he sings because God provides his need for food.

"But it's winter," the old man says. The robin replies cheerfully that even in the cold of winter, God always provides some crumbs to eat. The man grouses out a reply and shuts the window, but soon he is moved by the robin's joyful song and begins putting out crumbs on his sill for the robin to eat.

My friend, there is a reason that the Bible says, "Rejoice in the Lord alway" (Philippians 4:4). The only way to rejoice always is to rejoice in the Lord. Circumstances change, but God never changes.

Someone might say, "You can't be happy all the time." I agree. God doesn't promise that you will be happy all the time. It is not even His will that you be happy all the time, because happiness is temporary. It depends upon what happens. If your hap is good, you are happy; and if your hap is bad, you are unhappy.

But joy does not depend upon what happens. It comes from the Lord. Happiness is like a thermometer that registers conditions, but joy is like a thermostat that controls them.

Jesus wasn't happy all the time. He was "a man of sorrows, and acquainted with grief" (Isaiah 53:3). But Jesus had constant joy. On the night before He faced the cross, He used the word "joy" at least seven times in the Upper Room. He was going to die, but He said to His disciples, "These things have I spoken unto you, that my joy might remain in you, and that your joy might be full" (John 15:11).

Since today is a providential day, no matter what happens you can rejoice. There may be pain, but joy is there to help you bear it. A wise person once said, "Pain is inevitable, but misery is optional."

Do you want to have a great day every day? Accept today and each day as a gift fashioned by the hand of God. Learn to live in the eternal now. Today is the only day you have.

Stop saying, "If I only had time." You do have time. Stop fretting about yesterday and waiting for tomorrow, and start living today. Give God today, and He will make it a work of beauty. When you make every God-given day a God-governed day, it will be a God-gladdened day.

PART II

STANDING FOR TRUTH

7

Jesus the Truth

Why I Believe in Jesus

Shortly after the collapse of the Soviet Union and the end of Communist rule in Russia, I had one of the most challenging experiences of my life—the opportunity to preach in a marvelously beautiful hall in Moscow called the Red Army Theater.

This building is a theater for the performing arts, a magnificent structure with a big stage where operas and cultural events are held. I thank the Lord for the privilege of preaching in this theater. But I must also tell you that, even though spiritually I was trusting Him, quite frankly I was intimidated to be there.

One reason is the massive portraits of Vladimir Lenin and Joseph Stalin, the architect and the most brutal practitioner of Communism, that hang in the Red Army Theater. I could also look up and see the velvet box where they used to sit and listen to the performances. And if this wasn't intimidating enough, seated before me was a large audience of Red Army officers and their wives. These officers were decked out in their dress uniforms, sitting out there row upon row and rank upon rank.

As I looked out over that audience, I knew I was facing a tremendous challenge. Here were people who had been taught from their youth that there is no God. They were raised in an atheistic society; and not only that, but they had also most likely been raised to hate and distrust Americans. I wondered how much of that anti-God and anti-American training still lingered in the hearts and minds of these officers as they sat in that great auditorium built to glorify Communism.

I realized two things as I went to preach in Moscow that night. First, I realized that never again would I have an opportunity like this. And second, I realized that this would be perhaps the first and only time that many of these Red Army officers and their wives would hear a message from God's Word.

So I prayed and asked God, "Lord, what would You have me to say to these people?" And God the Holy Spirit said, "Adrian, tell them why you believe in Jesus Christ." And that's what I did, using as my text John 6:66-69, which describes what happened after Jesus made some statements that were hard to accept and a large crowd of would-be disciples began to thin out.

We will see that Jesus then turned to His twelve disciples and asked them a very penetrating question. Simon Peter stepped forward and answered with a question of his own. Then he made a ringing declaration that Jesus is the Son of the living God—the most important truth any man or woman could ever learn.

With this familiar story in John 6 before me, I said to those Russian officers in Moscow, "I want to tell you why I believe in Jesus Christ and why, along with Peter, I am sure that He is the Christ, the Son of the living God." I then gave them four reasons from John 6 to believe in Jesus.

In this chapter on "Jesus the Truth" I want to share these same four reasons with you. It is crucial that you know what you believe and why you believe it, because you are in a world filled with people who either do not believe in God or have never heard the clear message of Christ.

My hope is that the simple truths I am about to give you will reinforce your own faith and help you to "be ready always to give an answer to every man that asketh you a reason of the hope that is in you with meekness and fear" (1 Peter 3:15).

WHERE CAN WE TURN FOR TRUTH?

Before we get to these reasons, I want to set the stage for you just as I did in my message at the Red Army Theater. The sixth chapter of John opens with Jesus performing the great miracle of feeding five thousand men plus women and children. As a result, His popularity with the crowds was at an all-time high. The people had decided that anyone who could feed them like that would make a great king (see v. 15).

But Jesus knew what was in their hearts and withdrew. Crowds continued to follow Him, however, and He began to teach on the importance of eating His flesh and drinking His blood— that is, of partaking of Him. This message was so different, and so radical, that the people got offended and began to leave. We read what happened next in John 6:66-69:

> *From that time many of his disciples went back, and walked no more with him. Then said Jesus unto the twelve, Will ye also go away? Then Simon Peter answered him, Lord, to whom shall we go? thou hast the words of eternal life. And we believe and are sure that thou art that Christ, the Son of the living God.*

Peter asked Jesus a very penetrating question, which I also asked my audience in Moscow. "If you turn away from Jesus, where will you turn? Where can you go for truth if not to Jesus?"

The Emptiness of Atheism

I pointed out that some people turn to atheism, choosing to believe that in the beginning the heavens and the earth created themselves and then created man. I reminded these officers who had been steeped in godless teaching, "Atheism does not make sense. It is not a sign of intelligence." I reminded them that the true intelligentsia of past ages believed in God. Francis Bacon, Galileo, Sir Isaac Newton, Louis Pasteur, Albert Einstein, and Wernher von Braun all believed in God. Atheism has no answers that satisfy.

The Buttery Cloud of Philosophy

Then I asked my Moscow listeners, "If you don't turn to Jesus, will you turn to philosophy?" My friend, the world's philosophy is a system that tells us what we already know in words we can't understand. Dr. R. G. Lee, my predecessor at Bellevue Baptist Church, said, "Philosophy is a chunk of cloud bank buttered with the night wind." Study the great philosophers and see if philosophy satisfied their heart.

The German pessimist and philosopher Arthur Schopenhauer once said, "Life is a curse of endless craving and endless unhappiness." Aldous Huxley said concerning the human race, "It seems like we're a cancer on the globe." The English thinker Bertrand Russell didn't believe in God but said at the end of his life, "Philosophy proved a washout to me."

There are so many more philosophers and thinkers I could cite. H. G. Wells said, "Unless there is a more abundant scheme before mankind, this scheme of space and time is a bad joke, an empty laugh braying across the mysteries." Philosophy without God is an empty laugh and an empty wind.

The Futility of Materialism

Then I asked those Russian officers and their wives a third question: "If you reject Christ, will you turn to materialism for answers? Do you think that things can satisfy you?"

This question struck home because Communism and the Soviet empire were built upon a materialistic view of mankind. According to this view, people are nothing but machines whose only usefulness is to serve the state. But seventy-four years of Communism in Russia had demonstrated the futility of that view, and those Red Army officers could see it for themselves.

The futility of materialism was the subject when I visited the mayor's office in Moscow during my time there. I followed a red carpet, walked across marble floors, entered a big conference room, sat down with the leadership of the heart of Moscow, looked across the table at those men, and said, "Sirs, I want to tell you something. The Soviet empire has dissolved. Communism has crumbled. But if all you do is follow the West's economic ideas and nothing else, believing that capitalism is the answer rather than Communism, you will be disappointed."

Then I went on to explain, "Capitalism and Communism are just two forms of materialism, and they will never satisfy the deepest longing of your hearts. God made you for Himself, and even if you have material things, you will still find your hearts and lives empty without Him."

Those men nodded their heads. They had seen the inability of materialism to satisfy the heart.

The Dead End of False Religions

My final question to the audience in the Red Army Theater was this: "If you do not turn to Christ, will you turn to false religions?" Human beings are incurably religious, and many who turn away from Christ will turn to another religion.

But remember what Peter said to Jesus: "To whom shall we go? thou hast the words of eternal life." If you go to Confucius's grave, you will find it occupied. The same is true for Buddha, Mohammed, and every other so-called religious founder. But if you go to Jesus' grave, you will find it empty because He is not there.

You can still have Buddhism without Buddha. You can take Confucius out of Confucianism. You can take Mohammed out of Islam, and basically nothing has changed. But you can't take Jesus out of Christianity without destroying our faith.

Christianity is not just a creed, a code, a cause, or a church. It is a vital relationship with Jesus Christ. He alone has the words of eternal life. In Him dwells all the fullness and the wisdom of God. We can't turn to atheism, philosophy, materialism, or false religions and expect to find the truth. Only Jesus has the answer to the questions that really matter. Only Jesus can meet the deepest hunger of the human heart.

But this raises a question. How can we know that Jesus is really who He says He is? Why do we believe in Jesus? That night in Moscow I gave four reasons to believe in Jesus, and now I give them to you.

I BELIEVE IN JESUS FOR HISTORICAL REASONS

Jesus Christ is a fact of history. It doesn't matter whether you are a believer or not, you have to admit that a Man named Jesus was here upon this earth. Secular historians who have any merit at all admit the fact that Jesus Christ was a historical person, regardless of what they believe about Him.

The Evidence of History

In his *Outlines of History*, H. G. Wells listed Jesus Christ as number one on a list of the ten greatest men of history. All of history witnesses to the fact that Jesus was born in Bethlehem and lived a life unlike any other. His footprints are all over the pages of history. Each year is now called A.D., *anno Domini* or "the year of the Lord."

Jesus' birth divides history. Every time you put a date on a check or a letter, you're giving testimony to the fact that Jesus of Nazareth was here. Regardless of what you think about Him, He is a fact of history.

The Evidence of the Early Church

There's no way to explain the Christian church apart from the fact that Jesus Christ lived among us. The history of the early church also points to the reality of Jesus. The church not only taught that Jesus came to earth, but that He got up and walked out of the grave. The resurrection was the central truth of the preaching of the early church. They could preach with confidence because many eyewitnesses had seen Jesus after He was alive again.

Many theories have been put forth to dispute and disprove the witnesses to Jesus' resurrection, but none of them can stand up to close scrutiny. Someone may say, "The disciples were just hallucinating when they thought Jesus appeared to them." Well, He appeared to more than five hundred people at one time (1 Corinthians 15:6). But five hundred persons do not have the same hallucination.

Somebody else says, "They just saw a ghost, an apparition." But the Bible says Jesus' disciples ate with Him and touched Him (Luke 24:30; John 20:27).

A third objection is that the apostles and the early church deliberately lied about Jesus being raised from the dead. Do you really think so? We are talking about people who died for their faith in Jesus. A lot of people will live for a lie, but few will deliberately and willingly die for a lie if they know it to be a lie.

It has well been said that there is more proof that Jesus Christ rose from the dead than there is that Julius Caesar lived. You could put the name of almost any historical figure in that sentence, and it would still be true. The Bible says that Jesus showed Himself to be alive "by many infallible proofs" (Acts 1:3) that declare Him to be "the Son of God with power . . . by the resurrection from the dead" (Romans 1:4).

As He was speaking to the crowd in John 6, Jesus testified of Himself, "I came down from heaven" (v. 38). Jesus was here. That is an indisputable historical fact.

I BELIEVE IN JESUS FOR SCRIPTURAL REASONS

A second reason I believe in Jesus is because the Scriptures testify to the truth of His birth, death, and resurrection.

Jesus said, "No man can come to me, except the Father which hath sent me draw him: and I will raise him up at the last day. It is written in the prophets, And they shall all be taught of God" (John 6:44-45a). Earlier He had told the Jews, "Search the Scriptures; for in them ye think ye have eternal life: and they are they which testify of me" (John 5:39).

As I told those Russian officers, I believe in Jesus Christ because I believe the Bible is the Word of God. Now someone may say, "But, Adrian, that just moves the question back one step. To say that you believe in Jesus because you believe the Bible raises the question of whether the Bible is true."

That's a good point. But our faith in Christ and the Bible is not just circular reasoning. Let me give you five great proofs of the inspiration and truthfulness of the Holy Scriptures.

Five Proofs of the Bible's Truthfulness

The first of these proofs is *fulfilled prophecy*. So many hundreds of biblical prophecies have been fulfilled to the minutest degree that any chance of coincidence or happenstance is absolutely impossible. Neither is it possible for the Bible's supporters to have prearranged for these fulfillments. Fulfilled prophecy is an infallible proof of the Bible's truth.

A second proof of the Bible's veracity is *the wonderful unity of its theme and message*—humanly impossible for a book that was written over a span of fifteen hundred years by at least forty different authors on several continents in three different languages on all kinds of subjects. This unity would be impossible apart from supernatural revelation.

Related to this is a third proof, which is the Bible's *amazing longevity*. God's Word has not only lasted through the centuries, but it is still the most popular book in the world. Try reading last week's newspaper and see how stale and out-of-date it sounds. No other book has lasted the way the Bible has, and no other book has the power to draw people to it.

I saw this in Moscow when I reminded my audience that it used to be a crime to bring Bibles into Soviet Russia. Then I said I had a Bible to give everyone who was there that night, and they broke into applause. The Bible has lasted so long and has had such influence because it is "quick [or alive], and powerful, and sharper than any twoedged sword" (Hebrews 4:12).

The fourth proof has to do with the Bible's *scientific and historical accuracy*. I cannot survey this here, but there is an abundance of material on the subject that you can read for yourself. Suffice it to say that whenever the textbooks have been pitted against the Bible, God's Word has more than held its own. The history books have been revised, but not the Word.

The fifth and final proof I present to the truth of the Bible is its *undeniable power*. Jesus said to the crowd in John 6, "The words that I speak unto you, they are spirit, and they are life" (v. 63). The truths of God's Word transformed my life, and the numbers of people who could testify to the same transformation are legion.

The Bible Is the Story of Christ

Now if you read the Bible and you don't find Jesus Christ, go back and read it again. We read that Jesus called upon the prophets to give witness of Him (John 6:45). Acts 10:43 says of Jesus, "To him give all the prophets witness, that through his name whosoever believeth in him shall receive remission of sins."

How do the Scriptures testify of Jesus? First, they tell of His sinless, miraculous, virgin birth. Then they tell of His sinless, miraculous life. Jesus Christ is absolutely unique as He is presented in the Bible.

Think about the kind of Person the Bible presents Jesus to be. Jesus was a Man who never modified or withdrew any statement He ever made or apologized for anything He did. He never asked for advice from anybody, even though he walked among the Pharisees and scribes and doctors of the law.

Further, Jesus never troubled to justify His actions even when people misunderstood what He did, as when He delayed going to the home of His dying friend Lazarus (John 11:1-6). And it is very interesting that when His would-be disciples started deserting Jesus in John 6, He didn't try to dissuade them or run after them saying, "I'm sorry. I didn't mean to say that."

Jesus never confessed to a sin even one time and never had to ask forgiveness for anything. What an incredible life He lived. What strong points did Jesus have? In a sense none, because He didn't have any weak points! Every part of His life was in total harmony and symmetry.

The Bible also presents Jesus' sacrificial death. What was unique about the death of Jesus Christ is not that He died. Other martyrs have died. But He was the only Person who not only chose to die but chose the moment of His death (see John 19:30, which literally says, "He dismissed His spirit"). Listen to Jesus' own testimony: "No man taketh it [my life] from me, but I lay it down of myself. I have power to lay it down, and I have power to take it again" (John 10:18).

That last phrase refers, of course, to Jesus' resurrection, which came about through the power of God. The Scriptures present Jesus in all of His truth and glory, and no one has ever been able to explain Him away or discredit Him. I believe in Jesus for irrefutable scriptural reasons.

I BELIEVE IN JESUS FOR SPIRITUAL REASONS

Let me give you the third reason why I believe in Jesus Christ. I call this the spiritual reason because the truth is that with our human minds alone, we will never be able to comprehend who Jesus Christ really is. Unless the Holy Spirit quickens us and helps us to understand spiritual things, we will remain in the dark as to the truth about Jesus.

Jesus said to the crowd in John 6:63, "It is the spirit that quickeneth; the flesh profiteth nothing." Later Jesus told His disciples concerning the Holy Spirit, "He shall testify of me" (John 15:26).

The Twofold Witness of the Holy Spirit

The spiritual reason I am talking about here is the witness of the Holy Spirit to the truth of who Jesus is. The Holy Spirit will convict and convince you about Jesus if you truly want to know. This witness is both external and internal, as the apostle John explains in another book he wrote:

> *This is he that came by water and blood, even Jesus Christ; not by water only, but by water and blood. And it is the Spirit that beareth witness, because the Spirit is truth. For there are three that bear record in heaven, the Father, the Word, and the Holy Ghost: and these three are one. And there are three that bear witness in earth, the Spirit, and the water, and the blood: and these three agree in one.*
>
> —1 JOHN 5:6-8

Some people say to me, "Do you expect me to believe in Jesus Christ just because you say He was a proven figure in history or because your Bible says He died and rose again?"

My answer to that is no—I don't expect anyone to believe just because I say history and the Bible point to Jesus, though they do. It takes more than my testimony because anything I can talk a person into, somebody else can talk him out of. As a matter of fact, the Bible says that no one can believe without the convicting and convincing ministry of the Holy Spirit (1 Corinthians 12:3).

The Bible says in 1 John 5 that the Holy Spirit bears witness to the truth of Christ. We also need to see verse 9 of that chapter. "If we receive the witness of men, the witness of God is greater: for this is the witness of God which he hath testified of his Son."

Someone may object that he just cannot "just accept" the witness of the Holy Spirit concerning Jesus. But John says we receive the witness of men all the time, because the "if" in verse 9 could be translated "since." Somebody tells us something is true, and we believe it. We trust the pilot of our flight when he sits in the cockpit and claims to be able to fly the airplane. Every day we trust people we don't know and will never see again.

You Can Trust the Spirit's Witness

So if we trust fallible people, we can trust the witness of the infallible Holy Spirit. I challenged my audience in Moscow, "If you want to know who Jesus Christ is, ask the Holy Spirit." You see, God doesn't just say you must believe, but if you can't believe that's your hard luck. God says if you want to believe, He will help you understand and know that these things are true. Don't tell me you cannot believe once the Holy Spirit has revealed the truth to you. You may refuse to believe, but if you want to know the truth about Jesus, God the Holy Spirit will speak to you and confirm to you that Jesus is the Christ, the Son of the living God.

Verse 9 of 1 John 5 speaks of the Spirit's external witness. He also gives us an internal witness. "He that believeth on the Son of God hath the witness in himself" (v. 10). Why do I believe in Jesus? First of all because the Holy Spirit testified to me through the Word of God and through the evidence around me that "Jesus is the Son of God."

And now that I have received Jesus as my Savior and He lives in my heart, I have the witness in myself. You can argue with me all day long and never convince me against Jesus Christ. You can present sophisticated arguments to me, but I have the witness on the inside. And a Christian with the witness in his heart is never at the mercy of a man with an argument in his mouth. If you want to know the witness from within, accept the Bible's invitation: "O taste and see that the LORD is good" (Psalm 34:8). If you were to tell me that apple pie is not good or that there is no such thing as apple pie when I've just eaten a delicious piece, you can argue all you want, but I've got the evidence on the inside. I believe in Jesus for spiritual reasons because the Holy Spirit within me testifies to Jesus.

I BELIEVE IN JESUS FOR PERSONAL REASONS

The fourth reason I gave those Red Army officers for believing in Jesus is personal. Peter spoke to this dimension of the truth when he said to Jesus, "Lord, to whom shall we go? thou hast the words of eternal life. And we believe and are sure that thou art that Christ, the Son of the living God" (John 6:68-69).

Jesus Is Real to Me

Peter was saying, "I know the truth personally because I know Him who is Truth." History tells me that Jesus is the Son of God. The Bible tells me that Jesus is the Son of God. The Holy Spirit testifies to me that Jesus is the Son of God. And I know He is the Son of God through personal experience.

One time I prayed with a young man to receive Christ. He was searching for something real, and I will never forget his question. He looked at me and said, "Pastor, tell me—is Jesus real to you?"

I was able to say, "Yes, Jesus is real to me. I am sure that He is the Christ, the son of the living God."

Paul said, "I know whom I have believed, and am persuaded that he is able to keep that which I have committed unto him against that day" (2 Timothy 1:12). The best people I know know Jesus personally. The best people I know love Him.

I have met a lot of people in my ministry, including some false disciples, hypocrites, and imposters. Many of those in the crowd following Jesus in John 6 probably fit one of those descriptions. But when you meet God's wonderful people you can see how He changes lives and what He means to them. I believe in Jesus because He lives within my heart, and I know that I know that I know He is my Savior.

I had a dear friend whose name was Byron Richardson. Byron and his wife were driving through the Smoky Mountains on vacation, having a wonderful time. It was getting late in the evening on that mountain road when Byron's wife said, "Sweetheart, we had better get some gas in the car. It's getting late."

In typical male fashion, Byron replied, "It's all right. We have plenty of gas. I'll stop in time. Don't worry about it." She drifted off to sleep, and Byron was driving that beautiful road when night fell. The needle on the dashboard went almost to Empty, and he began to look for a gas station. But they were on a mountain road, it was dark, and there was no gas station in sight.

Byron knew he was in deep trouble. "She told me to get gas and I didn't," he said to himself. "If we run out of gas on this mountain road, I don't know what she will do to me." So he began to pray, "Lord God, please, I need gasoline."

Then when it seemed that he was burning vapors, he saw a little grocery store. The lights were shining through the window.

It was open, and out front was an old-fashioned gasoline pump that looked like it might be an antique rather than an active pump.

Byron took a deep breath and went inside to ask if the store sold gasoline. The mountaineer-grocer nodded his head and said, "Yep" and walked outside. Byron began to praise the Lord as the old mountaineer began to fill his tank. Byron was so overcome with relief that he stood up straight and stretched, took a big whiff of mountain air, and said to the grocery store owner, "It's great to be alive, isn't it?"

Byron said the old man never even lifted his head as he replied, "I don't know. I ain't never been no other way."

Well, I have been some other way. Once I was dead in trespasses and sins, but Jesus has radically, dramatically changed my life. That's one way I know He is the Son of God.

Make Sure Jesus Is Real to You

I said to the officers that night in the Red Army Theater in Moscow, "These are the reasons I believe in Jesus, and I want to ask you to believe in Him too." I asked them to bow their heads as we prayed the sinner's prayer. Then I said, "If you prayed that prayer and asked Christ into your heart, would you lift up your hand?" It looked to me as if more than half of those men lifted their hands, indicating they had prayed to receive Christ as their personal Lord and Savior. Hallelujah!

We have good reasons to believe in Jesus. Where else can we go—He alone has the words of eternal life? My prayer is that you are convinced beyond a shadow of a doubt that Jesus is the Christ, the Son of the living God. And I pray that believing, you have found life in His name.

8

The Gospel Truth

The Best News Ever

A seminary professor of mine from other days told me a story about a mother whose son was missing in action during World War II. The young man was declared dead, and his mother received the news that every mother dreaded the most.

But then the War Department found out that her son was not dead at all, but alive and well. The department asked my former professor, Dr. Roland Leavel, who was a pastor in the community, to go see this mother with the joyous news, "Your son is alive."

Imagine how excited you would be to go to a mother who thought her son was dead, knock on her door, and say, "I have good news for you!" That's how excited we ought to be about preaching the gospel of Jesus Christ, because we have better news to deliver than my professor had to give that mother. Our good news is that Jesus Christ has conquered death, the grave, hell, and judgment, and we can live forever with Him!

The gospel is the best news that a lost and dying world could ever hope to hear. Some form of the word *gospel*, which literally means "good news," is used over ninety times in the New Testament. Paul's great declaration of the gospel in 1 Corinthians

15 begins with these words: "Moreover, brethren, I declare unto you the gospel which I preached unto you, which also ye have received, and wherein ye stand; by which also ye are saved, if ye keep in memory what I preached unto you, unless ye have believed in vain" (vv. 1-2).

Paul is preparing to give his readers the heart of the gospel message that he preached, and there are three wonderful things about the good news of Christ that I want us to see in this passage. But before we display this sparkling diamond, we need to do what a jeweler does when he shows a diamond to a potential buyer. We need to spread out a dark background to display the gospel against so that it will shine even more radiantly.

THE DARK BACKGROUND OF OUR SINS

This dark background is the fact of our sins. What is it that makes good news good? The thing that makes good news so good is the nature of the bad news. Our sin is the black velvet upon which the diamond of God's grace, the good news of the gospel, dazzles so brilliantly. Paul writes, "For I delivered unto you first of all that which I also received, how that Christ died for our sins" (1 Corinthians 15:3).

Those last two words are the bad news. "Our sins" are the reason Jesus Christ had to die. "For all have sinned, and come short of the glory of God," Paul wrote in Romans 3:23.

The reason the gospel is not good news to many people is that they refuse to believe the bad news of sin. The world has worked overtime to explain away sin. People put all kinds of spins on their sin to keep from having to face the truth.

We hear corrupt business executives, shady politicians, and philandering athletes say they made an error, a mistake, or a misjudgment. They might even confess to a weakness, but not to sin. More sophisticated types might try to call sin a psychological maladjustment or glandular malfunction for which people are not responsible. But no matter what we call sin today, we've just taken the old poison and put new labels on it.

There is a school of psychology called behaviorism, which teaches that we human beings are nothing more than the sum total of our bodily chemistry and environment. Given a certain stimulus, we respond the way a dog salivates when food is put in front of him. You can't blame a person for his glandular response any more than you can blame the dog for its response.

You may not hear the term *behaviorism* much these days, but the concept is firmly embedded in modern man's psyche. Those of us who lived in the sixties saw this mechanical view of man in action in the "Great Society" programs our government enacted to wipe out poverty.

That system, which actually created more poverty and despair, was built on the premise that given the right environment, human beings would react the right way. Thus, since thieves only stole because they were raised in bad surroundings and poverty, the answer to crime was to provide people with jobs and housing, and former criminals would become model citizens.

Now I'm not saying that people don't need decent housing and meaningful work. But that theory proved to be an utter failure, and our nation is still paying a heavy price for the fallout. But that hasn't stopped liberals in politics, humanists in psychology, and evolutionists in science from putting forward their explanations to deny sin. The liberals say we can legislate problems like crime and greed out of existence by throwing enough money after them and passing new laws.

To the humanists, a person may be weak but not wicked, sick but not sinful. Everybody's ill, but nobody's evil, because we can find justification for any action if we dig back far enough.

The evolutionist says sin is a non-category because the human race is still evolving and progressing upward. Any flaws are just holdovers from a previous stage of evolution that will someday be bred out of the race as we progress upward from the primordial soup from which life spontaneously arose.

That's a pretty dark background against which to display the dazzling diamond of the gospel, wouldn't you agree? But the part of this background that gets my hackles up more than any of these things is when a preacher stands in the pulpit and tries to explain away sin.

I'm afraid the examples of this are legion. Over the years I have heard of pastors who dismissed sin as a problem of environment, bad experiences in childhood, or a tool of fear that the church uses to keep the faithful in line. One pastor said, "Paul's words that 'Through one man sin entered into the world, and death by sin' can be dismissed as nonsense."

That man ought to get out of the pulpit and make an honest living. Sin is public enemy number one. It is a clenched fist in the face of God. Sin is hellish and damnable. The Bible says, "For the wages of sin is death" (Romans 6:23). Paul made this charge in Romans 5, which the preacher I quoted above called nonsense: "Wherefore, as by one man sin entered into the world, and death by sin; and so death passed upon all men, for that all have sinned" (v. 12).

I've never met a person brazen enough to stand up and say, "I've never sinned." But I've met plenty of people who say, "Well, yes, I've sinned—but I've never robbed a bank or committed murder!"

But the Bible says, "For whosoever shall keep the whole law, and yet offend in one point, he is guilty of all" (James 2:10). What does that mean? How many of the Ten Commandments do you have to break to be a sinner? Not all ten, but just one, as James went on to make clear by his example in verse 11.

Here's a man dangling over a fire by a chain of ten links. How many links in that chain have to break before he falls into the fire? Just one. Now we divide sins into categories. The "small" sins are things such as telling a "little white lie," taking a few supplies home from the office, or stealing change from our father's dresser when we were little.

These things may seem small in our eyes, but they are an indication of a much bigger problem deep in the human heart. The problem is not what a man does, but what he is. A man is not a thief because he steals. He steals because he's a thief. He tells lies because he's a liar. Jesus said, "Out of the abundance of the heart the mouth speaketh" (Matthew 12:34).

There is a fatal flaw in human nature called sin, and if we don't deal with it, it will kill us and then send us to hell. Until you admit the bad news of sin, the gospel will never be good news to you.

THE SOURCE OF THE GOSPEL

Now with this background in place, we are ready to display the beauty of the gospel—the best news ever heard—as Paul records it in 1 Corinthians 15:1-4.

I want to begin by talking about the source of the gospel. Paul deals with this beginning in verses 3-4: "For I delivered unto you first of all that which I also received, how that Christ died for our sins according to the Scriptures; and that he was buried, and that he rose again the third day according to the Scriptures." The source of the gospel is the death, burial, and resurrection of Jesus Christ.

Paul says this truth is of first importance, which is the meaning of the phrase "first of all." This is not a statement of time, but of timelessness. Paul wants us to know there is nothing more important he has to say than that the gospel finds its origin in Christ's death, burial, and resurrection, which were according to the Scriptures.

Now if the bad news is sin, how does the gospel as revealed in Jesus deal with sin? The good news is that the gospel addresses every area of our need when it comes to sin.

The Gospel Deals with the Penalty of Sin

Part of the bad news of sin is that it brings with it a penalty. The cross was God's judgment against sin. "The soul that sinneth, it shall die" (Ezekiel 18:4) is the verdict of heaven's court. We just read above that the wages, or payment, of sin is death.

When Jesus died on the cross, He made full payment for our sins. When the Bible says He died for our sins, it is saying that He died "on behalf of" our sins. That is, Jesus died to pay our sin-debt.

The Bible says Jesus died according to the Scriptures. You see, our Lord's death on the cross was not an incident, accident, or afterthought. It was in accordance with the written Word of God, which in Paul's day was the Old Testament. Seven hundred years before Jesus Christ came into this world, the prophet Isaiah wrote, "All we like sheep have gone astray; we have turned every one to his own way; and the LORD hath laid on him the iniquity of us all" (Isaiah 53:6).

Our sins were laid upon the Lord Jesus Christ, who took them to the cross and shed His precious blood to make full payment. And just before He died, Jesus cried out from the cross, "It is finished" (John 19:30). This was a wonderful proclamation, meaning literally "paid in full."

You see, a holy God demands that sins must be paid for. God cannot simply overlook or ignore sin, for if He were to do that, He would be an unjust judge and no longer holy. God could not simply say, "I forgive you" without exacting a penalty for sin.

Suppose a man was found guilty of a heinous, horrible crime, but the judge said, "Oh well, that's all right. We all make mistakes. I'm going to do the loving thing and let you go free."

A judge who did that would be removed from the bench. In a court of law when a guilty man is acquitted, the judge is condemned. If God knowingly and deliberately overlooked sin, then He would topple from His throne of holiness. The Bible says, "The LORD . . . will not at all acquit the wicked" (Nahum 1:3). Sin must be paid for, but Jesus Christ died for your sins and mine so that we would not have to pay for them with eternal death in hell. The debt is paid in full!

The Gospel Deals with the Pollution of Sin

Sin not only brings a penalty, it also brings pollution to the soul that sins. Our problem is not just the punishment that our sin deserves. Our problem is what sin has done to us on the inside.

The gospel addresses the problem of sin's pollution when Paul says in 1 Corinthians 15:4 that Jesus was buried for our sins. Along with the full and free pardon of our sin, there is also the purging of our sin.

Often when we hear the gospel being taught or discussed, the emphasis is put upon Christ's death and resurrection. Praise God for that, but Paul says Jesus' burial is part of the first importance of the gospel. Why does the apostle emphasize Christ's burial?

The first reason is that the Lord's burial proved that He really died. Jesus was sealed in that grave for three days and three nights. He was truly dead. This is important because if Jesus did not really die on the cross, then our sin has yet to be paid for.

You may say, "Adrian, does anyone really doubt that Jesus actually died? Is that something we need to emphasize?"

My friend, the fact is that there have been people throughout history who have tried to deny the reality of Jesus' death. Like other theories we have talked about that try to deny Christ, these views don't hold water, but they have been put forth from time to time.

One of these ridiculous ideas was that Jesus only fainted on the cross; this is called "the swoon theory." The people thought He was dead; so they buried Him and rolled a huge rock over the door of the tomb. But in the coolness and dampness of the tomb, Jesus revived, shook off the effects of His wounds and the flogging that tore the flesh from His body, unwrapped Himself from the grave clothes wound tightly around His entire body, rolled the one-and-a-half to two-ton stone from the door of the tomb, either overpowered or scared off the entire Roman guard of up to sixteen soldiers, then went out and conquered the world!

Believing something like this takes more faith than it does to believe that Jesus died and rose again. Jesus was buried because He was dead. The main reason Paul includes the burial of Jesus Christ in the gospel is what it signifies—which is the removal of the pollution of sin.

I said above that part of the sin problem is what sin has done to pollute us on the inside. When you get saved, Jesus makes your heart clean. The defilement, the pollution of sin is put in the grave of God's forgetfulness.

Jesus Christ's being buried helped signify that He had become sin for us (2 Corinthians 5:21). When Christ was put into that grave, your sin was buried with Him out of God's sight, just as a dead person is put away out of sight.

Jesus not only forgives us in the judicial sense of pardoning our sins, but He cleanses us on the inside. "Though your sins be as scarlet, they will be as white as snow; though they be red like crimson, they shall be as wool" (Isaiah 1:18). Your sins are buried in the grave of God's forgetfulness. That's what the act of baptism pictures. We are buried with Christ in baptism, which pictures the removal of sin's pollution. You never have to be haunted by the ghost of guilt again. The old person you used to be is dead and buried.

The Gospel Deals with the Power of Sin

The good news of the gospel just keeps getting better, and this may be the best part of all. "[Jesus] rose again the third day according to the Scriptures" (1 Corinthians 15:4). Jesus rose triumphant over sin and broke the back of Satan. He has demolished the power of sin. The writer of Hebrews says Jesus came that "he might destroy him that had the power of death, that is, the devil" (2:14).

It was sin that nailed Jesus to the cross and laid Him in the tomb. But now He has risen. God the Father raised Jesus from the dead as His final stamp of approval on His Son. Jesus' enemies had tried Him in a mock trial, accusing Him of being a blasphemer, a fraud, and a troublemaker. Their verdict was that Jesus was worthy of death. So they crucified Him.

Oh, but that was a lower court's ruling. A higher court, the heavenly court where God the Father sits as Supreme Judge of the universe, reversed that lower court's decision. God said, "They were wrong, and I am going to raise up My Son to demonstrate that I have accepted His payment for sin."

Peter said in his sermon on the Day of Pentecost, "[Jesus], being delivered by the determinate counsel and foreknowledge of God, ye have taken, and by wicked hands have crucified and slain: whom God hath raised up, having loosed the pains of death: because it was not possible that he should be holden of it" (Acts 2:23-24).

God raised Jesus up in reversal of the judgment made against Him by wicked men. The Bible says in Romans 4:25 that Jesus "was raised again for our justification." The resurrection proved that God was completely satisfied with Jesus' sacrifice.

We saw in a previous chapter that only ignorance scoffs at the fact that Jesus lived on this earth. Paul wrote that Jesus is "declared to be the Son of God with power . . . by the resurrection from the dead" (Romans 1:4). Beyond the shadow of any doubt Jesus walked out of that grave and showed Himself alive with many infallible proofs.

Now before we leave this subject, let me give you a little Greek lesson that will make this truth even richer. The verbs Paul used in 1 Corinthians 15:3-4 for "died" and "buried," referring to Jesus, are both in what is called the aorist tense in Greek. This is a verb form that means a fact accomplished, something that happened at one point in the past and is over. Jesus died and was buried only once. He will never die again.

But when Paul said that Jesus "rose" from the dead (v. 4), that's a different story altogether. The literal sense is that Jesus "has been raised." This verb is in the perfect tense, which in Greek specifies past action with continuing results in the present.

In other words, Jesus was raised from the dead by the Father two thousand years ago, and He is still raised and alive today. More than that, He is raised for all eternity. Jesus is risen and always will be risen.

That means you're never done with Jesus. You can deny and refuse Jesus and die without Him, but you'll rise in the judgment of the lost, and there sitting on the throne will be Jesus Christ. He is risen. That's what the gospel is all about. It is God's good news about the bad news of sin.

The Force of the Gospel

The gospel of Jesus Christ has a glorious source in the death, burial, and resurrection of Jesus Christ. But the gospel also has a glorious and powerful force that does amazing things for all those who are saved by it.

An unbelieving anthropologist was once visiting a primitive tribe in the jungles of Asia to whom missionaries had brought the gospel. The anthropologist was talking with the chief of the tribe, questioning whether the message of Christ could possibly have any impact on his people, or whether it was even necessary for them.

But the chief disagreed strongly, saying that the gospel had definitely made its power felt among his people.

"How do you know that?" asked the anthropologist.

"Because," the chief replied, "if we were not Christians we would have eaten you by now." Hallelujah for the force of the gospel that can turn warriors into worshipers. Besides, they probably would have gotten indigestion anyway from eating a bitter old infidel!

The Gospel's Saving Force

I see at least three ways that the gospel of Jesus Christ makes its power felt in our lives. The first of these is the gospel's saving force. In 1 Corinthians 15:2, Paul said it is that "by which also ye are saved."

There is no other way to be saved apart from the gospel. That's why Paul said, "I am not ashamed of the gospel of Christ: for it is the power of God unto salvation to every one that believeth" (Romans 1:16). The gospel has the power to save anyone—from the professor in the university to the headhunter in the jungle.

Our job is to protect and proclaim the truth of Christ's saving power, not to alter it or try to make it more acceptable to a politically correct world. Notice what Paul said after declaring the gospel's power: "if ye keep in memory what I have preached unto you" (1 Corinthians 15:2). He's not talking about memorizing Bible verses here. "Keep in memory" means "to hold fast" to the gospel—not to change, amend, or embellish it. The gospel is gloriously simple and simply glorious.

The Gospel's Sanctifying Force

The gospel also has a sanctifying force that is sometimes the overlooked and underappreciated aspect of Christ's work.

Don't be fearful of the word *sanctification*. It simply means to be set apart or dedicated to a specific purpose. Sanctification is the Bible's term for the power of Christ to keep you saved. The gospel's sanctifying force is suggested by the present tense of the verb "are saved" in verse 2 above. Because the present tense in the Greek language denotes continuous action, this could be translated, "by which you are being saved."

Now you may say, "Wait a minute, Adrian. I thought I was already saved. Have I been saved, am I being saved, or will I be saved?"

The answer is yes! You see, the gospel saved us from the penalty of sin, it is right this moment saving us from the power of sin, and one day when Jesus returns to take us to heaven, we will be saved from the very presence of sin.

So the gospel continues to work. Maybe you have seen the sticker that says, "Please be patient with me. God isn't finished with me yet." That's pretty good theology on a bumper. God is doing His work of salvation in us, sanctifying us or making us more like Jesus Christ. And He will continue His work until we are with Him. I have His promise on that: "He which hath begun a good work in you will perform it until the day of Jesus Christ" (Philippians 1:6).

Salvation is a crisis whereby you come to God and say, "I am a sinner. Forgive my sin, come into my heart, and save me," and He does. This crisis is followed by a process whereby God continues to work in you day by day, conforming you to the image of Christ (Romans 8:29).

The gospel's sanctifying force is what gives us the power to obey the command, "Grow in grace, and in the knowledge of our Lord and Saviour Jesus Christ" (2 Peter 3:18). As one Bible teacher used to say, we will either grow in grace or groan in *disgrace*. We can grow because the gospel has the power to keep us every day.

The Gospel's Stabilizing Force

The truth of the gospel's stabilizing force grows naturally out of its saving and sanctifying force. Going back to the first verse of 1 Corinthians 15, we read these words: "I declare unto you the gospel which I preached unto you, which ye also have received, and *wherein ye stand*" (emphasis added).

I love this. It is good news that we can be saved. It is better news that we can be saved and know it. It is glorious news that we can be saved and know it, and know that once we are saved we can never lose it. This is the doctrine of the believer's security forever in Christ.

Put it down big and bold. When you get saved you don't keep Christ—He keeps you. There is a wonderful promise in Romans 14 that ought to bless you. Paul had a question for believers in Rome who were going around criticizing and judging others in the church: "Who art thou that judgest another man's servant? to his own master he standeth or falleth. Yea, he shall be holden up: for God is able to make him stand" (v. 4).

Do you know what God is actually saying here to people who look at a poor, stumbling believer and decide he will never make it? God is saying, "Mind your own business! That man is My servant, and I am going to hold him up. He will stand because I will make him stand."

Don't let anyone rob you of the confidence of your security in Christ. And don't let anyone convince you that salvation is probation, that God gives you a fresh start and then stands back to see if you can make it. I wouldn't trust the best fifteen minutes I ever lived to get me to heaven.

One of the best proofs that we are secure in Christ forever is that the Bible speaks of eternal life in the present tense, as if it were already an accomplished fact. John says, "These things have I written unto you that believe on the name of the Son of God; that ye may know that ye have eternal life" (1 John 5:13). Whatever else it may be, eternal life that isn't really eternal isn't good news.

The good news is that you're saved and kept by the grace of God. I want to tell you, I stand assured and amazed in the keeping power of God. And I'm in good company because Paul stood there too. "By the grace of God I am what I am," he wrote (1 Corinthians 15:10). You may tremble on the Rock, but the Rock will never tremble under you. This is the stabilizing force of the gospel.

THE COURSE OF THE GOSPEL

Here is the reason I love being a gospel preacher. The good news of Jesus Christ extends to every person in every place and addresses every problem that we could ever face.

The Gospel Extends to Every Person

What a glorious message we have to deliver. I can look at anybody anywhere on the face of the earth and say, "No matter who you are or what you have done, if you trust Jesus He will save you. 'For whosoever shall call upon the name of the Lord shall be saved'" (Romans 10:13).

Does that mean a murderer, a rapist, or a blasphemer can be saved? Yes, it does. It also means so-called good people can be saved, because in God's sight "there is none righteous, no, not one" (Romans 3:10).

I love the story of the British noblewoman who told the great evangelist John Wesley that she was saved by the letter *m*. When Wesley asked her to explain, she said, "The Bible says not many noble are called. It doesn't say not any are called."

The apostle Paul didn't have any illusions about who or what he was before he came to Christ. He called himself the "chief" of sinners and "less than the least of all saints" (1 Timothy 1:15; Ephesians 3:8). But don't stop there, because he also said, "His grace which was bestowed upon me was not in vain" (1 Corinthians 15:10).

The Gospel Flows to Every Place

You don't have to be in church to be saved, because the gospel reaches to every place. We hear from many people who listen to our ministry over radio or television, or even by tape at a later date, and receive Christ as their Savior.

If you can show me any place at the farthest end of the earth where the gospel cannot reach, or if you can introduce me to anybody anywhere who is beyond the saving grace of Christ, then I will close my Bible and never preach again.

The Gospel Covers Every Problem

There is also no problem that the gospel does not address. You may say, "Adrian, you don't know my problem." Well, I can reduce them all very simply. Every problem we human beings have is a subcategory of either sin, sorrow, or death.

The gospel is the only answer to sin, for it offers full pardon and a place in God's forever family.

The gospel is the only answer to sorrow, for even though we

may weep we have Jesus' promise, "Your sorrow shall be turned into joy" (John 16:20).

And praise God, the gospel is the only answer to death, for again our Lord has promised, "I am the resurrection, and the life: he that believeth in me, though he were dead, yet shall he live: and whosoever liveth and believeth in me shall never die" (John 11:25-26). The Bible says, "The last enemy that shall be destroyed is death" (1 Corinthians 15:26).

Someone has imagined a little procession of caterpillars crawling along the ground sadly, carrying the cocoon in which their brother used to live. But he's gone now, and they're going to have a funeral for him.

Above this sad little scene is a beautiful butterfly with his wings shimmering in the sunlight. He's the former caterpillar being mourned down below, but he is free and complete, enjoying what he was made to be.

This is your destiny in Christ, dear reader. You have nothing to fear, because in Christ you are as saved and secure today as you will be one million years from now in glory. There is no good news like the gospel!

9

Fallen Truth

Snake Eggs, Spiderwebs, and Traffic Jams

Our beloved United States of America is in a crisis today. Even before the unthinkable happened on September 11, 2001, we were deeply engaged in a battle for the heart and soul of this great nation. During the nineties the lights of decency and of hope were being blown out one by one, and yet it seemed that Americans were content to see morality compromised and to elect scoundrels to office as long as they gave us prosperity.

But the prosperity bandwagon began to run off the road early in 2000 when greed and speculation reached their limit and the Internet bubble burst, taking the market down with it. Then we were rocked back on our heels by revelations of corporate greed and dishonesty on a scale no one could have conceived. As I write this, things are still so bad economically that a recent headline in one major city's newspaper told how there were no jobs available for students because all the out-of-work adults had taken them.

But it is not economics that concern me so deeply. "Experts" say the market will turn around eventually because it always does. My burden is for the moral and spiritual collapse in America that has pushed our country to the very edge of God's judgment.

Consider the recent Supreme Court decision legitimizing sodomy by striking down Texas's anti-sodomy law. I believe history will rank this unconsionable decision alongside the infamous *Roe v. Wade* ruling of 1973 that legalized abortion with its destructive influence on this country. The question in the case of this decision on homosexuality is whether America will have another thirty years of history from which to look back on it.

This country is in deep trouble, and we cannot sit back and wait for things to turn around. I thank God for leaders at the national, state, and local levels who seek to honor Him and do what is right. But we are far beyond the place where we can elect our way back to righteousness in America.

If something dramatic does not happen to bring our great country back to God, the day will come when we will face terrorism or some other calamity more horrific than anything we have seen. We will fill our churches, turn our eyes upward, and dial heaven's 911, but the line will be dead. People will cry out, "O God, have mercy!" But there will be no answer. Why is that?

I believe the answer is found in Isaiah 59:1-14, a passage that needs to be proclaimed from every pulpit and shouted from every rooftop in this land. The prophet writes: "Behold, the LORD's hand is not shortened, that it cannot save; neither his ear heavy, that it cannot hear: But your iniquities have separated between you and your God, and your sins have hid his face from you, that he will not hear" (vv. 1-2).

BARRIERS BETWEEN A HOLY GOD AND A SINFUL PEOPLE

Isaiah was saying to a sinful nation of that day that God was neither crippled nor deaf. The problem was that the people's sins had created a barrier between them and a holy God. As Isaiah detailed God's charges against the people and revealed the sin of that day, take note of how their perverseness parallels the sin of our day.

We Live with Bloody Hands

God's first charge is in verse 3a: "For your hands are defiled with blood, and your fingers with iniquity." America is swimming in an ocean of blood. A modern holocaust called abortion continues to stain this nation. The blood of tens of millions of pre-born babies cries out from the ground against us, ever since 1973 when the Supreme Court decided that a pre-born baby could be treated as a piece of tissue and eliminated.

The price we are paying for the slaughter of our babies is horrendous. Do you suppose there is a correlation between the fact that children and young people are being gunned down in the streets of America, and even being killed by their own parents, while several thousand unborn babies are killed each day in abortuaries?

The epidemic of murder in our land is a judgment from God for the legalized murder of abortion. As long as we allow the blood of innocent babies to flow in private in America's abortion mills, should we be surprised at the blood that flows in the streets and in our homes?

If you ask the politicians about abortion, most will hide their faces from it and dodge the issue. Or if they speak out, it is more often than not in defense of the barbarity. Just recently we listened to the lunacy of a U.S. senator from California suggesting that a baby was not really viable and worthy of protection until it was taken home from the hospital!

The politicians say abortion is a personal decision between a woman and her pastor, priest, or rabbi, and not a proper subject for politics. But if a religious leader speaks out about abortion, the politicians and pundits rise up and say, "He needs to stay out of politics." And meanwhile the babies die.

One man has said, "We're living in a day when twelve-year-olds are having babies, fifteen-year-olds are killing each other, and eighteen-year-olds are graduating from high school with diplomas they can't read." That's where we are in America today as our bloody hands betray our sin.

We Speak with Lying Lips

But Isaiah was just beginning God's indictment of the people of Israel. The prophet continues in verse 3: "Your lips have spoken lies, your tongue hath muttered perverseness."

During the 1990s we became so used to hearing lies from Washington that it seemed as if everybody was lying. And there didn't seem to be much embarrassment about it. We were witnessing a startling disregard for basic honesty, and it filtered down to the people. I'm not saying that all lies originated from Washington, but the atmosphere of those years helped set the tone for the nation.

It wasn't long before a string of news reports came out about high-profile public figures who had lied on their résumés to help win their positions. Several resignations followed amid pleas of "I made a mistake." But these faded into the background when it was discovered that top officers in one of America's prestigious corporations were lying to their own employees and to the public about the company's true financial condition.

Earlier in his prophecy, Isaiah had delivered the Lord's word of judgment to a nation whose attitude was this: "When the over-flowing scourge shall pass through, it shall not come unto us: for we have made lies our refuge, and under falsehood have we hid ourselves" (28:15).

The Lord God replied to this arrogance, "Judgment also will I lay to the line, and righteousness to the plummet: and the hail shall sweep away the refuge of lies, and the waters shall overflow the hiding place" (v. 17). God is saying, "I am sick of the lies."

Theodore Roosevelt, a man known for rock-ribbed honesty, won his first major election in 1898 when he became governor of New York. About that time, Roosevelt wrote something that's so pertinent it sounds like it was written for today:

> No community is healthy where it is ever necessary to distinguish one politician among his fellows because he is honest. Honesty is not so much a credit as an absolute prerequisite to efficient service to the public. Unless a man is honest, we have no right to keep him in public life. It matters not how brilliant his capacity. It hardly matters how great his powers of doing great service on certain lines may be. If a man lies under oath or procures the lie of another under oath, if he perjures himself or suborns perjury, he is guilty under the statute law. Under the higher law, under the great law of morality and righteousness, he is precisely as guilty if, instead of lying in a court, he lies in the newspaper or on the stump and in all probability, the evil effects of his conduct are infinitely more widespread and more pernicious. The difference between perjury and mendacity is not in the least one of morals or ethics; it is simply one of legal forums.

Roosevelt was saying that lying lips, a lack of straightforwardness and honesty, should immediately disqualify a person for public service. Jesus said, "Let your communication be, Yea, yea;

Nay, nay: for whatsoever is more than these cometh of evil"
(Matthew 5:37). Someone who has to call a press conference to
clarify or withdraw his previous denial is not speaking from an
honest heart.

We Scheme with Wicked Hearts

Here's a third charge God made against ancient Israel that parallels modern-day America: "None calleth for justice, nor any pleadeth for truth: they trust in vanity and speak lies; they conceive
mischief, and bring forth iniquity" (Isaiah 59:4).

It's terribly hard to raise children today because we live in a
day of moral ambivalence and ethical fogginess. Our young people are being told that premarital sex and couples living together
before or without marriage are normal and expected behav-
iors. And the kids are getting the message! A new poll shows that
70 percent of young people between the ages of thirteen and sev-
enteen believe it's all right for a couple to live together before
marriage.

You say, "Yes, Adrian, things certainly are bad out there in the
world." Things aren't much better in the church, judging from this
same survey. *Fifty percent* of those who identified themselves as
church kids voted that cohabitation before marriage is acceptable.

At least these young people are being forthright about their
beliefs. Every recent study of church young people reveals that in
terms of ethical behavior such as cheating or lying, teenagers
who claim to be Christians are virtually indistinguishable from
their non-church peers.

What has happened? We are raising a generation of Americans
for whom truth is decided by personal convenience, and unques-
tioning tolerance of any and all views is the only virtue. Well-

known youth speaker Josh McDowell said that thirty years ago when he presented the claims of Christ to a college audience, the students challenged him to prove the truth of his message. But he said that when he speaks to students today, their response is, "Who do you think you are to make such narrow-minded claims?"

These ungodly attitudes are the disturbing products of a society in which "none calleth for justice, nor any pleadeth for truth." When a famous professional athlete stood before the cameras and denied rape charges by saying that his only guilt was adultery, the reaction was mocking laughter among the late-night comics and a "So what?" attitude in general.

Our society says adultery is no big deal. Everybody does it. We Americans had already decided by the way we voted in the nineties that a man's private morality had nothing to do with his public service. But I want to tell you, if a man will not keep a sacred vow before Almighty God to his wife, I wouldn't trust him to keep any promise anywhere, anytime.

God's Word says, "Dead flies cause the ointment of the apothecary to send forth a stinking savour: so doth a little folly him that is in reputation for wisdom and honour" (Ecclesiastes 10:1). Something stinks in America today.

The sweeping gains being made by the homosexual movement today are a perfect example of the lie we are being told that public approval is the measure of whether behavior is wrong or right.

But this same prophecy of Isaiah warns, "Woe unto them that call evil good, and good evil; that put darkness for light, and light for darkness; that put bitter for sweet, and sweet for bitter!" (Isaiah 5:20). No amount of public opinion or judicial bullying can turn darkness into light or a lie into the truth.

What brought about this condition among the people of Isaiah's day? How did they get to the place where they looked up to God and cried, "Have mercy on us," but God said, "No, I am not going to hear your prayers"? What brought about their bloody hands, lying lips, and wicked hearts? Learn the answer from Scripture, and you will see what is wrong in America today.

PROBLEM NUMBER #1:
SNAKE EGGS: FEEDING ON A DIET OF DECEPTION

The first problem with the people of Isaiah's day is that they had been feeding on a diet of deception. "They hatch cockatrice' [viper's] eggs, and weave the spider's web: he that eateth of their eggs dieth, and that which is crushed breaketh out into a viper" (Isaiah 59:5).

This is a graphic picture of what is hatched in hell's incubators. Those viper's eggs are devilish lies and philosophies that were being hatched in Isaiah's day and are also being hatched in our day. They are lying, poisonous philosophies being swallowed by adults and youth alike.

Our nation is on a snake-egg diet, a diet of deception. The incubators that hatch those eggs are materialism, humanism, New Age-ism, and liberalism. The old granddaddy serpent who has spawned and fertilized these eggs is Satan himself because he is a liar and the father of lies (John 8:44).

Certain philosophical underpinnings are so incipient in American life today that they are poisoning our educational, philosophical, religious, and political outlook. Our young people in public schools are being served a snake-egg omelette every morning, and they are swallowing it down.

I heard one recent example of this that would have been

unthinkable just a generation ago. A Christian woman hosted her high-school-age niece and several friends for a week. Wanting to see where these young people were coming from in terms of their moral views, she engaged them in conversation with several leading questions. It quickly became evident that for these kids, pretty much everything was up for grabs morality-wise.

That became apparent when in the course of their discussion, the Nazi Holocaust against the Jews came up. This woman said she was shocked to hear her niece say that even though the Holocaust might seem wrong to us, it wasn't necessarily wrong for the Nazis because they really believed that what they were doing was right. When the woman asked her niece how she came to that view, she said she learned it from her teacher in school!

How do you answer that kind of moral perversion? The woman telling the story is an accomplished Bible teacher, but she said she was stunned into speechlessness for a few moments.

Can there be any doubt that dramatic changes have taken place in America over the past forty years? Look at the reversals that took place in just one twenty-year span, from 1962 to 1982.

In 1962 the Supreme Court ruled that voluntary prayer in public schools was unconstitutional. They told us our children had to be in the public schools, but they couldn't pray there. In 1963 the same court dismantled classroom Bible reading. There is no room for the Bible in our halls of education.

Then in 1980 the posting of the Ten Commandments in schools was declared unconstitutional. Students who were plotting to bring guns to school and kill their classmates were not allowed to read, "Thou shalt not kill" lest it prejudice and corrupt them. Finally, in 1982 the courts prohibited the teaching of biblical creation in schools. In twenty years God was expelled from our public schools and told not to return.

And what have we reaped from this in the past twenty or so years? Well, a school-based clinic can't give a child an aspirin without parental permission. But there are still many places in America where a teenage girl can receive abortion counseling and birth control devices at her school's clinic without her parents' knowledge or approval. And she can go out and get the actual abortion with the same "right to privacy."

Our children are being served a diet of deception in school. Prayer is out, policemen are in. Bibles are out, values-free education is in. The Ten Commandments are out, but cheating and immorality are in. Creation instruction is out, evolution and blind chance are in. Corporal punishment is out, disrespect and rebellion are in. Traditional values are out, unwed motherhood is in. Abstinence is out, condoms are in. Learning is out, and social engineering is in. History is out, and revisionism is in. All of this, and worse, is possible when people are taught that they are the product of blind mechanical forces instead of being created in the image of God.

For example, ever since the Nazi Holocaust the commitment and cry of the Jewish people has been, "Never again!" And until recently, the world confidently believed that we had progressed far beyond such barbarity.

But the massacres in places like the former Yugoslavia and Rwanda have shattered that illusion. And just as frightening is the fact that when people begin to believe an evil like the Holocaust wasn't "necessarily wrong," the stage is set for a repetition. When the people of Babel came together to defy God and build the first one-world system, God said, "Now nothing will be restrained from them, which they have imagined to do" (Genesis 11:6). And God judged them.

Now here's the sad thing about viper's eggs. Isaiah said that not only do those who eat the eggs die, but "that which is crushed breaketh out into a viper." When you come against these evil things and try to stamp them out, all you do is create more snakes. To try and stamp out these snake eggs of devilish deception is not the answer.

PROBLEM NUMBER #2:
SPIDERWEBS: WEAVING A WEB OF WICKEDNESS

Now someone could argue that many people in America are not feeding on this diet of deception served up largely by the schools and our popular culture. But we also need to watch out for the web of wickedness, the second problem that makes our nation a nation in crisis.

We see this also in Isaiah 59:5, where we are told that the people "weave the spider's web." You may know that spiders weave a web that is almost invisible and very sticky. The purpose is to catch an unsuspecting insect that will fly into the web and become entangled. The spider comes over, kills its prey with a sting, wraps the victim in more strands, and leaves it hanging there until the spider is ready to feed on it and suck it dry.

A friend who had just moved to the country said he opened his back door one night to go outside, only to be confronted with a huge spiderweb that covered half the doorway. He decided not to challenge the spider, so he shut the door. As he stood inside admiring the web, an insect flew into it. My friend watched in amazement as the spider ran to its victim, killed and wrapped it in a matter of just seconds, then ran back to another part of the web to await its next meal.

What a picture of the way Satan works. He has woven webs of immorality and dishonesty that are poisoning and sucking dry a generation of young people today. But he has also woven another "web" that is entangling not only young people but countless numbers of men—the worldwide web of online pornography that is invisible yet incredibly sticky. And just as a spider can snare and bag a victim within seconds, so even a fleeting first glance at pornography on the Internet can snare a person.

I am weary in my soul of the arguments over whether viewing pornography in private does any harm. The question always comes up, does pornography lead to degeneracy? What a foolish question. Pornography *is* degeneracy! Our children can go home to an empty house, get on the Internet, and watch unspeakable things as they access pornographic sites. Husbands and fathers log on at night as they hide their sin from their families. And Satan draws the web ever tighter.

The devil also has his web of drugs and alcohol, a deadly trap. America is filled today with the walking dead whose lives have been sucked dry by the spiders of alcohol and drug abuse. But to whom are the advertisements for these things directed? Largely to our young people. Binge drinking by college students has become such a problem that several universities have implemented new policies to curb it. This is commendable, but we are working on the wrong end of the problem. Someone needs to curb the producers of this poison instead of just the consumers.

Some years ago a popular series of beer ads showed attractive people doing something enjoyable like fishing. One of the men would hoist the sponsor's beer, smile, and say to his friend, "It doesn't get any better than this."

Let me tell you something. They were right! Alcohol never gets any better. It always gets worse.

Then there is the sticky web of immorality. Young people are being told today there are no fixed standards of right or wrong when it comes to sexual expression. As I said above, faithfulness in marriage is grist for the talk show comics and is constantly denigrated on the television sitcoms.

And in so-called sex education classes in many of our schools, the threefold goal is teach children how to fornicate without guilt, without catching a disease, and without conceiving a baby. A representative of Planned Parenthood said their sex education program did not make value judgments and was based on the assumption that since kids are going to be sexually active anyway, they need information on how to act responsibly.

How would you like your little girl to go to school and be taught that she shouldn't try to pin labels of "good" or "bad" on people's sexual behavior, whether it is premarital sex, promiscuity, bisexuality, or homosexuality? Would you be concerned if she came home saying that morality is individual or just an outmoded concept from your generation? Get concerned, my friend, for that is what millions of boys and girls are learning.

May God have mercy upon us when we tell our children that prayer, God's Word, and the Ten Commandments are too "narrow" and "bigoted" to be seen or heard in school! The devil is weaving his webs of wickedness across this nation, and people are falling headlong into them.

But just as the answer to viper's eggs is not to try and stamp them out, the answer to webs of wickedness is not just to sweep them down, because like a spider's web they will be back by morning. Something more is needed to eradicate these things.

PROBLEM NUMBER #3:
TRAFFIC JAMS: TRUTH FALLEN IN THE STREETS

But now we come to the reason for the terrible situation America is in. Truth has been dumped into the street like the trash beneath our feet. Moving on in Isaiah 59, we read:

> *For our transgressions are multiplied before thee, and our sins testify against us: for our transgressions are with us; and as for our iniquities, we know them; in transgressing and lying against the LORD, and departing away from our God, speaking oppression and revolt, conceiving and uttering from the heart words of falsehood. And judgment is turned away backward, and justice standeth afar off: for truth is fallen in the street, and equity cannot enter. Yea, truth faileth; and he that departeth from evil maketh himself a prey.*
>
> —VV. 12-15A

This last phrase really strikes home with me because I have learned over the years that when you stand up and speak against the moral decadence of our nation, you become the bad guy. When you call for justice and truth, the world portrays you as a villain. That's where we have come today.

Notice that the prophet said there is a traffic jam in the streets where truth is concerned. Truth, justice, and equity are trying to enter the city, but they cannot because truth is fallen, and all of the traffic is backed up.

Now please take note that truth is not dead. You can't murder the truth. You can kill its messengers, but truth is eternal because it comes from the eternal God.

But what has caused truth to fall and lie prostrate on the ground? Truth has been knocked down in America by doctors of philosophy who deny God. She has been tripped up by politicians who sell their principles for popularity and by corporate executives who trade honesty for luxury. And truth has been chloroformed by liberal preachers who dilute and distort the truth they purport to proclaim.

So here is truth, lying fallen in the streets. May I say with all of the unction, function, and emotion of my soul, the job in America today is to put truth back on her feet!

There is not a lot wrong in this country that could not be put right quickly and dramatically if in pulpits all across America a generation of preachers would open the Book of Truth and preach, "Thus saith the Lord God Almighty" without fear.

Truth would also be lifted up if the people in this nation who truly know Jesus Christ as their Savior would determine that in their homes, their schools, and their places of business, truth will prevail whatever the cost.

My friend, we have all the access we need to all the truth we will ever need. The Bible in our hands is the Word of Truth. The Holy Spirit who lives within us is called the Spirit of truth. Jesus said of Himself, "I am the truth." The church is called "the pillar and ground of the truth" (1 Timothy 3:15).

We can get facts from many sources, but there is a difference between facts and truth. Knowledge may double, but truth will never double because it is fixed and eternal. Truth is to your heart what food is to your body, light is to your eyes, and melody is to your ears.

When we think about the crisis of morality and truth in America, most of us want to get out there and start stamping out snake eggs and knocking down spiderwebs. But what we need is something that will slay the snake and destroy the spider—and that is truth.

Only truth can keep the daddy serpent, Satan, from spawning more eggs. Only truth can keep that spider from weaving sticky webs. We need to lift up truth in America today and put her back on her feet where she belongs, at the very center of our society.

I call upon you as a believer to rededicate yourself to the truth of God. Teach your children to live the truth, to love the truth, to tell the truth, to know the truth, and to believe the truth. "Buy the truth, and sell it not" (Proverbs 23:23).

There is a prize to possess, which is truth, but there is also a price to pay to possess it. You must study God's truth, pore over it, know it, and live it. And you must preserve the truth. Don't let anybody take the truth from you. The early Christians did not argue over the Bible. They loved it, believed it, expounded it, and poured it forth as white-hot lava.

Person by person, family by family, church by church, and city by city, we've got to take America back. My heart is broken over snake eggs, spiderwebs, and traffic jams. There is only one thing that will set America free from these traps. Jesus said, "Ye shall know the truth, and the truth shall make you free" (John 8:32). Buy the truth, and cherish it.

10

Standing with Truth

Truth or Consequences

Our radio and television ministry, Love Worth Finding, is a member of the National Religious Broadcasters (NRB), the premier organization of those who seek to minister God's Word through the broadcast media.

The NRB holds a national convention each year, and at one of these gatherings I was asked to bring the keynote message on the convention's theme, which was "An Unchanging Message to a Changing World." There were some four thousand broadcasters, station owners, television people, and religious leaders in the audience that night. I want to share with you the basic message I delivered to the National Religious Broadcasters, because we still face the need to proclaim an unchanging message to a changing world.

Much as I did when preparing to speak to the Russian army officers I told you about, I asked the Lord what He would have me say to this large organization of Christian broadcasters whose purpose was to stand for truth. He led me to 1 Kings 22.

What we have in this chapter is the story of a good man named Jehoshaphat. He was the king of Judah who tried to do a good thing. But he was a good man who did a good thing the wrong way because he got himself in league with an ungodly man whose name was Ahab, the king of Israel. Let's turn to the story from the Word of God:

> *And they continued three years without war between Syria and Israel. And it came to pass in the third year, that Jehoshaphat the king of Judah came down to the king of Israel. And the king of Israel said unto his servants, Know ye that Ramoth in Gilead is ours, and we be still, and take it not out of the hand of the king of Syria? And he said unto Jehoshaphat, Wilt thou go with me to battle to Ramoth-gilead? And Jehoshaphat said to the king of Israel, I am as thou art, my people as thy people, my horses as thy horses.*
>
> —vv. 1-4

Ahab said, "Ramoth-Gilead belongs to us, not to Syria. Why are we just sitting here? Let's go get it back." And Jehoshaphat immediately answered Ahab, "I'm with you."

No prayer. No seeking the face of God. Here was a good man who made an unholy political alliance with a wicked man, and he was about to reap the consequences. Jehoshaphat was like many people today who plan, plot, and agree, and then after they've done it, they carry it to God in prayer and ask Him to rubber-stamp their plans.

That's what happened here. "And Jehoshaphat said unto the king of Israel, inquire, I pray thee, at the word of the LORD to day" (v. 5). Jehoshaphat said, "You know, we ought to pray about this thing. We need a word from God." Now remember, he's already made up his mind. He's already given his word and entered into an alliance, and now he tries to get God to rubber-stamp it.

That old wicked king Ahab had filled his court with four

hundred of his own paid, pussyfooting, pandering prophets, whom he called together. "Then the king of Israel gathered the prophets together, about four hundred men, and said unto them, Shall I go against Ramoth-gilead to battle, or shall I forbear? And they said, Go up; for the Lord shall deliver it into the hand of the king" (v. 6).

Here were four hundred preachers speaking with unanimity. Now Jehoshaphat knew that something is really wrong when four hundred preachers get together about anything. So he was getting a little nervous and said, "I'm suspicious of this." So he said to Ahab, "Is there not here a prophet of the LORD besides, that we might inquire of him?" (v. 7).

Now notice verse 8: "And the king of Israel said unto Jehoshaphat, There is yet one man, Micaiah the son of Imlah, by whom we may inquire of the LORD: but I hate him; for he doth not prophesy good concerning me, but evil. And Jehoshaphat said, Let not the king say so."

Ahab said, "I don't want that preacher around here. He never says anything good to me or about me. He never prophesies good concerning me." Of course he couldn't. How can you say anything good to or for a bad man? Micaiah was God's man. But Jehoshaphat said, "King Ahab, give Micaiah a chance. Let's hear what this 401st prophet will say." So they sent for Micaiah because Ahab needed Jehoshaphat, and he didn't want to lose that cooperation.

The messenger who was sent to bring Micaiah told him, "Behold now, the words of the prophets declare good unto the king with one mouth: let thy word, I pray thee, be like the word of one of them, and speak that which is good" (v. 13).

This envoy began to butter Micaiah up. "Now look, Micaiah,

don't mess this thing up. We've got absolute unanimity. Four hundred prophets have said we ought to go to war against Syria and take Ramoth-gilead. Make it unanimous. Vote with the ministerial alliance."

Now we come to Micaiah's glorious answer, which is key to everything else I said to those religious broadcasters that night, and is key to what I want to share with you in this chapter. The answer that this man of God gave has put steel in my backbone, and I pray that it will do the same for you as you commit yourself to stand for the truth.

"And Micaiah said, As the LORD liveth, what the LORD saith unto me, that will I speak" (v. 14). That's underscored in my Bible.

Micaiah was declaring, "It may not be pleasant, but I'll say whatever the Lord says to me. It may not be prudent, but I'll say it. It may not be pleasing, but I'll say it. It may not be profitable, but I must say it. I may go to jail [and Micaiah did, by the way], they may even kill me, but I'll say it. I may not get a promotion, but I will say it. I will not be intimidated by the king. The king can't put strings on me."

Do you know the difference between a puppet and a prophet? A puppet has strings on it. But no man of God can have strings on him. Micaiah said, "What God says to me, that I will say." Now with that in your heart, let me give you five statements that I pray will be true about you and me as we stand for truth.

1. It is better to be divided by truth than to be united in error.

Now I must be very careful here as I say this, because Christian unity is a wonderful thing. And we must do everything we can do to keep the unity of the church and to be one with all of our brothers and sisters in Christ. The Bible tells us in Ephesians 4:3 that we are to be "endeavoring to keep the unity of the Spirit in the bond of peace." And the psalmist wrote, "Behold, how good and how pleasant it is for brethren to dwell together in unity!" (Psalm 133:1).

But our unity must only be that which the Spirit can say amen to, because the Bible says in Amos 3:3, "Can two walk together, except they be agreed?" There are some things you just can't put together, and there is no cook skilled enough to make a good omelette out of bad eggs. Unity in the Holy Spirit—yes. Unification and uniformity that sacrifices truth—no. We must learn this lesson from the Scriptures.

> *Be ye not unequally yoked together with unbelievers: for what fellowship hath righteousness with unrighteousness? and what communion hath light with darkness? And what concord [or agreement] hath Christ with Belial? or what part hath he that believeth with an infidel? And what agreement hath the temple of God with idols? for ye are the temple of the living God; as God hath said, I will dwell in them, and walk in them; and I will be their God, and they shall be my people.*
>
> —2 CORINTHIANS 6:14-16

Jehoshaphat was trying to be unequally yoked together with Ahab. Ahab was a wicked unbeliever, while Jehoshaphat was a believer.

Let me tell you something. Not only is Jesus Christ the great unifier of all those who believe in Him, but He is also the great divider. Jesus is the most divisive Person and His teaching the most divisive force that ever hit Planet Earth.

There is a lot of sentimental preaching about Jesus being the great unifier, but Jesus has caused more division than any other force since creation. These are His own words about Himself, which may surprise you: "Think not that I am come to send peace on earth: I came not to send peace, but a sword. For I am come to set a man at variance against his father, and the daughter against her mother, and the daughter-in-law against her mother-in-law. And a man's foes shall be they of his own household" (Matthew 10:34-36).

Many Christians could testify, "That is true in my house. Ever since I gave my heart to Christ there's been strife and division in my house concerning the Lord Jesus Christ." Those who value unity above truth have missed the Spirit of Jesus. It is better to be divided by truth than united in error.

Martin Luther led the Protestant Reformation, a movement that broke with the ungodly uniformity of his day. Here's what the mighty reformer said:

> I do not want to know anything of peace and concord when the Word of God is thereby lost and the Word and eternal life and everything is forfeited. It is not right for me here to draw back and give way out of love toward you or toward any other man. But before the Word everyone must give way, whether he be a friend or an enemy. For the Word has not been given to us for the sake of external or worldly concord or peace, but for the sake of eternal life. Don't talk to me, therefore, of love and friendship if the Word and faith are to be compromised.

We remember Martin Luther today because he paid a price and took a stand. What you and I call the Protestant Reformation was actually a great revival meeting. Luther also said, "The Bible does not state that love brings us everlasting life, God's grace, and all of the heavenly treasures, but the Word brings them to us."

Many historians say that the greatest preacher who ever lived, outside of the apostle Paul, was Charles Spurgeon. Here's what Spurgeon had to say about false unity: "Where union and friendship are not cemented by truth, they are an unhallowed confederacy."

Too bad Jehoshaphat didn't know this. Too bad Jehoshaphat somehow joined himself up with an unholy man in the person of the wicked King Ahab. It is better to be divided by truth than to be united in error. Our unity is in Christ and Christ alone.

Now please understand. I am not asking God's people to divide over incidentals. But when the great, eternal values of the Word of God are jettisoned and crucified upon the altar of conformity and cooperation, it is a sin against Almighty God.

2. It is better to speak the truth that hurts and then heals than to tell a lie that comforts and then kills.

Those four hundred hired prophets in Ahab's court told him and Jehoshaphat a lie. The spokesman made horns of iron and told Ahab and Jehoshaphat, "Thus saith the LORD, with these shalt thou push the Syrians, until thou have consumed them. And all the prophets prophesied so, saying, Go up to Ramoth-gilead and prosper: for the LORD shall deliver it into the king's hand" (1 Kings 22:11-12).

This was a lie that Ahab loved because these pandering preachers told him what he wanted to hear rather than what he needed to hear. And as a result, he fell in a great calamity.

Preachers need to stop trying to win popularity contests and instead tell the truth no matter how much it hurts, because only truth can ultimately bring healing. Micaiah told Ahab the truth, but Ahab said, "I hate the message this man brings." He saw a man who was his friend as his enemy.

The former pastor of the church where I serve, Dr. Robert G. Lee, used to say when he preached on hell, "Some will call preaching about hell cruel. But I'd rather be called cruel for being kind than to be called kind for being cruel." Rough truth is better than polished falsehood.

The Word of God tells us, "It is better to hear the rebuke of the wise, than for a man to hear the song of fools" (Ecclesiastes 7:5). Some people today in our churches are hearing the song of fools. There is a view current in some circles that says if you want to attract people to your church, don't say anything on Sunday morning that might offend them. Don't preach on judgment, hell, or separation from the world. If you do preach on these things, we are told, this generation of people will be turned away. Keep it general.

One well-known preacher who has a large church and national television audience once said it was crude, destructive to human personality, and counterproductive to evangelism to try and make people aware of their lost and sinful condition before God.

Many preachers today are calling people to come to Jesus if they need a friend or someone to help them with their problems or make them happy. Now Jesus is the greatest Friend of all, and He cares about our deepest needs. But people don't just need a friend or problem-solver. They need a Savior. They need to know that they're lost. They need to know that they are sinners under the wrath of a righteous and holy God.

That's not a popular message. But it is better to tell the truth that hurts and then heals than to tell a lie that comforts and then kills.

A group of sailors went to a chaplain and asked him this question: "Chaplain, do you believe in hell?"

He said, "Yes, I do. Why do you ask?"

They said, "Because if there is a hell and you don't believe in it, we don't want you for a chaplain. And if there is no hell, we don't need any chaplain." There is a hell, the wrath of God is real, and someone had better be telling lost people the truth about it.

Micaiah refused to be bought or intimidated. When he stood before Ahab, he spoke the word that God had given him concerning the battle Ahab and Jehoshaphat were going out to fight: "I saw all Israel scattered upon the hills, as sheep that have not a shepherd: and the LORD said, These have no master: let them return every man to his house in peace" (1 Kings 22:17).

Micaiah gave Ahab the prophecy of his death. Ahab would have been wise to heed it, but he was too proud and arrogant. All four hundred of the other prophets had glibly decreed victory for Ahab. But Micaiah refused to be a part of this ungodly unity, even though his was the only voice of dissent.

My friend, you cannot build a work of God that will last without telling the truth. I don't believe that we ought to go out of our way to be rude to people. And I have told the people at our church in Memphis that we must be loving, warm, and friendly, we must have a servant attitude, and we must make the last the first and the lowest welcome.

But it is not my job to fill the pews of our church. It is my job to fill the pulpit. It is not my job to make the message palatable, but to make it profitable, to preach the Word of God. The truth may hurt, but it also heals. A lie comforts and then kills.

The Word of God puts it this way: "Open rebuke is better than secret love. Faithful are the wounds of a friend; but the kisses of an enemy are deceitful" (Proverbs 27:6). What Ahab was receiving was four hundred deceitful kisses from faithless prophets who had never heard from God, rather than hearing the wound of a friend, Micaiah, a man who wanted to tell him the truth.

3. It is better to be hated for telling the truth than to be loved for telling a lie.

Ahab had said of Micaiah, "I hate him" (v. 8). Why? Because Micaiah told Ahab the truth. And Ahab said this even before Micaiah prophesied this wicked king's defeat and death in the upcoming battle at Ramoth-gilead. Ahab had four hundred puppet prophets on his string, but Micaiah wouldn't dance to the king's tune.

I hope it is not a shock to you to learn that every servant of God is not going to be loved. Now I want to be loved. I don't like to be disliked. But it is better to be hated for telling the truth than to be loved for telling a lie.

Micaiah was a man of God. He wasn't campaigning for Clergyman of the Year. We who proclaim God's Word have to stop running for popularity contests. The apostle Paul would not give way when he told the Galatians that they were in doctrinal error. Then he asked them this question: "Am I therefore become your enemy, because I tell you the truth?" (Galatians 4:16). Somehow we think today that those who tell us the truth are our enemies.

I heard about a man whose family sent him to the doctor because he constantly complained of being too sick to work. The doctor examined his patient, then told him to get dressed and meet him in his office.

When the man came into the office and sat down, he said, "Give it to me straight, doc. Don't use any complicated, fancy-sounding medical terms. My family wants the truth in plain English. What's wrong with me?"

"All right," the doctor said, "I'll make it as plain as I can. There isn't a thing wrong with you. You're just lazy."

The man sat silent for a moment, then said, "I see. Now will you give me a complicated, fancy-sounding medical term I can tell my family?" Many people don't want to hear the truth.

I was driving to an engagement one time in south Florida. The sun was shining, I had a good rental car, I was on a very fine road, and beautiful music was playing on the radio. I was having a wonderful time, praising the Lord as I sailed along listening to the music.

But as I drove on, I got a suspicion that something was wrong. I wasn't seeing the signs I needed to see to get to my destination. So I stopped and asked a highway patrolman, "Is this the way to thus and such?"

He said, "Mister, you're headed the wrong way, and you're far from where you ought to be."

Let me ask you a question. Was that officer who told me I was on the wrong road an enemy or a friend? After all, I was enjoying myself on the wrong road. He brought me bad news, but had he not told me the truth, the news would have been much worse farther down the road. I made my engagement because someone told a man on the wrong road in a good car listening to beautiful music on a sunny day, "You're headed the wrong way." Paul's question to the Galatians is the question of the hour for the twenty-first century church: "Am I your enemy because I tell you the truth?" Micaiah told the truth, and they put him in prison on a bread and water diet (1 Kings 22:27).

A friend in a former church called me one Monday. She said, "Pastor, were you preaching to me on Sunday?"

I said, "I was shooting down in a hole. If you were down in it, I can't help it." I loved her, but she was wrong, and she knew it.

We're not called to be loved by everybody but to bear the reproach of Jesus. As a matter of fact, if you'll study the Bible it is impossible to find anybody who stood for the truth and yet was loved by everyone.

Abel was killed by his brother. Noah was so hated that he could not get any converts other than his family in 120 years. Joseph was sold into slavery. Moses was hated and ridiculed by his family. Elijah was chased by this same Ahab and his she-devil of a wife named Jezebel until he thought he was the only true prophet left. Elisha was called a baldhead. Isaiah preached to deaf ears. Jeremiah wept because of the recalcitrance of those he preached to. Daniel was put in a lions' den. His Hebrew friends were thrown into the fiery furnace. David was chased and hunted by Saul. John the Baptist lost his head for telling King Herod he was an adulterer. Peter was crucified upside down. Stephen was stoned. Paul was left for dead outside Lystra. John the apostle was exiled on Patmos. James the brother of John was martyred. And the Lord Jesus Christ was crucified for telling the truth.

Dear reader, I wish I could assure you that if you stand for the truth, you will be hailed as a hero. But I must be honest and tell you that the only hail you may receive is a hail of angry looks, angry words, or maybe worse. Let's just be sure that if we suffer for our words, it is for telling the truth and not for passing along slander or gossip.

The apostle Peter said, "Let none of you suffer as a murderer, or as a thief, or as an evildoer, or as *a busybody in other men's matters.* Yet if any man suffer as a Christian, let him not be ashamed; but let him glorify God on this behalf" (1 Peter 4:15-16, emphasis added).

4. It is better to stand alone with the truth than to be wrong with a multitude.

Consider 1 Kings 22:13-14 again. "The messenger that was gone to call Micaiah spake unto him, saying, Behold now, the words of the prophets declare good unto the king with one mouth: let thy word, I pray thee, be like the word of one of them, and speak that which is good. And Micaiah said, As the LORD liveth, what the LORD saith unto me, that will I speak."

That is, "I'll not make it unanimous. I don't care what those four hundred preachers say. I'm going to say what God says." And it turned out 400 to 1.

I've learned in life that the majority is almost always wrong. As a matter of fact, the majority is almost always wrong in our churches. The majority of the people don't come to prayer meeting. The majority don't come to Sunday night worship. The majority is generally, and almost always, wrong.

There is a drive today toward a spirit of uniformity that will homogenize society, downplay differences, and obliterate conviction. But remember that the Antichrist is working to build a one-world church in a one-world state. The religion of America today is "get-alongism." We're almost considered un-American if we don't put our arms around everybody's shoulder and say, "Your religion is just as good as mine."

To say that Jesus Christ is not a way or the best way to heaven, but the *only* way is to brand you as a narrow-minded bigot. To declare that the Bible is the inerrant Word of God is to invite the charge of being uncooperative and—horror of horrors—a fundamentalist. They say it's lonely at the top. Well, it's lonely with the truth too.

But then, men of God have always stood alone. I mentioned

Noah, who had to stand alone when he preached. Elijah stood alone on Mount Carmel against the four hundred and fifty prophets of Baal. Amos stood alone in the courtroom at Bethel. True prophets must stand alone.

The yes-men at Ahab's court tried to soften Micaiah up. "Come on, Micaiah," they said, "we've already taken a vote, and it's 400 to 0. Your vote won't count anyway if you go against the prophets. All it will do is get the king upset, and then we'll be in trouble. So just vote with the ministerial alliance, and everything will be fine."

But Micaiah cast his vote with God and split the phony unity. I want to say again that we must not divide over incidentals in the body of Christ, but we must stand for conviction even if we have to stand alone.

Sometimes we may have to stand alone even in our church or our own denomination. As I write this, one of the mainline Protestant denominations in America has just elected its first openly homosexual bishop, and the Bible believers in that group are weighing their response.

In my own denomination there are those who say, "Now wait a minute, Adrian. All Southern Baptists are conservative if you compare them with the rest of Christianity. If you draw a line down the center of all Christendom, even the most liberal Southern Baptist would be to the right of that line."

My response to that is, so what? You can draw a line anywhere and put anybody on either side of it. It just depends on how far you move the line and what group you're dividing.

You may have heard about two brothers who were wicked, ungodly, lascivious men. They were perverts, adulterers, drunkards, thieves, brawlers, blasphemous—you name it.

One of the brothers died, and the other brother came to a preacher and said, "I will give you a thousand dollars if you will preach my brother's funeral and call him a saint."

The preacher said, "You've got a deal."

At the funeral, with the living brother sitting up front, the preacher stood up and pointed to the deceased. "The man in this casket was a liar, a thief, a drunkard, a pervert, an adulterer, and a blasphemer. But compared to his brother here, he was a saint."

You see, you can make anyone appear saintly if you move the line far enough. The news media are always trying to portray any difference in convictions over the truth of God's Word as a difference between the right and the left. But as I once told a reporter for ABC News, it is not a matter of right or left. It is a matter of right or wrong. If you make truth a matter of right or left, then you can draw a line anywhere.

But if you take the Word of God and say, "What God has said, that will I say," then it's not right or left. It doesn't matter what your particular persuasion happens to be. The issue is what God has to say. In America we need to come to a fixed standard, not of conservative versus liberal, but of the Word of God versus everything else.

I'll be accused of "pro-Western bias" for this, but I'm still of the conviction that as the West goes, so goes the world. And as America goes, so goes the West. And as Christianity goes, so goes America. And as evangelicals go, so goes Christianity.

I thank God that the Southern Baptist Convention is saying, "We are not trying to fall in line with the rest of the mainline denominations. We are taking a stand for the inerrant, infallible Word of God." Our leaders have been taking a beating in the media, and even from some within, for this uncompromising stand.

But I believe God's Word is worth the struggle, even if we have to stand alone. We are the largest Protestant denomination in the world, and if we don't stand for truth we will take a lot of churches and people down with us when we fall.

Not only do denominations and churches have to stand alone, but families have to stand alone too. If you are in a church that doesn't take a stand for the Word of God, then you need to get your family into another church.

You say, "But I've been a member of this church for so long. And besides that, my grandmother is buried in the church cemetery in the backyard." Well, I'll guarantee you, Grandma would leave if she could!

Sometimes individuals have to stand alone. You may be the only one in your family who stands for the truth. Again, don't divide over incidentals. Paul's advice in this area was, "If it be possible, as much as lieth in you, live peaceably with all men" (Romans 12:18). But it is better to stand alone with the truth than to be wrong with a multitude.

5. *It is better to ultimately succeed with the truth than to temporarily succeed with a lie.*

Micaiah's word from the Lord was fulfilled when Ahab went into battle. We read, "And a certain man drew a bow at a venture, and smote the king of Israel between the joints of the harness: wherefore he said unto the driver of his chariot, Turn thine hand, and carry me out of the host; for I am wounded" (1 Kings 22:34). Ahab died that same evening.

And what about our friend, good King Jehoshaphat? He got far more than he bargained for because Ahab convinced him to go into battle wearing his kingly robes while Ahab disguised himself. In other words, Jehoshaphat had a big target painted on him, and when the Syrians saw him, they mistook him for Ahab and attacked him. Jehoshaphat ran away, crying out that he wasn't their man, and the Syrians stopped the attack (vv. 30-33).

Jehoshaphat should have run away screaming, with his hands over his ears, earlier in Ahab's court when he heard Micaiah's prophecy and saw him punched in the mouth and dragged off to prison for telling the truth!

It was a tragic battle for Ahab. He would not listen to the man of God and the Word of God. The preacher was thrown in prison. But God's arrow found Ahab, and God's crown has found Micaiah. It is better to ultimately succeed with the truth than to temporarily succeed with a lie.

I want to give you the same closing word I gave to that assembly of the National Religious Broadcasters. We need to be people of God who will buy the truth and not sell it. We need to remember that truth is desperately needed in today's world. And we need to remember that truth is not some vague concept that no one can pin down. Rather, "The word is nigh thee, even in thy mouth, and in thy heart" (Romans 10:8).

The Bible contains the precepts of truth. Jesus is the Person of truth. And the Holy Spirit is the power of truth. I reminded my fellow broadcasters, and I remind you now, of what former president Woodrow Wilson said: "I had rather temporarily fail with a cause that must ultimately succeed than to temporarily succeed with a cause that must ultimately fail."

11

Inward Truth

*A Boy with a Slingshot and a
Giant with a Sword*

We have seen some wonderful biblical examples and stories
of people who stood for truth no matter what. But I have
kept back, if the not the best, then certainly the most familiar story
for last as we close these studies.

I want to review with you the story of a young boy who had
great strength against a powerful enemy because his heart was
pure. And I want you to see that his purity came from his integrity,
or inward truth, because this boy trusted in God with all of his
heart. Later in his life he confirmed what he had learned in his
youth when he said to the Lord, "Behold, thou desirest truth in the
inward parts" (Psalm 51:6).

You may know by now that we are going to consider an event
from the life of David that is one of the best known stories in the
Bible. As we follow David out to confront the Philistine giant
Goliath, we will see how knowing and acting on the truth can help
us deal with the giants in our lives.

We all have giant-size problems: cruel circumstances that have
threatened us and our loved ones; Goliath-like enemies of temptation, fear, jealousy, covetousness, discouragement, heartbreak,

or financial reversal that cause many of God's people to live lives of quiet desperation.

But I want to say that God's plan for His children is victory always and in every circumstance. Now don't think this is just "preacher talk." I'm telling you on the authority of God's Word that His plan for His people is victory in every circumstance.

Paul declared, "Now thanks be unto God, which always causeth us to triumph in Christ" (2 Corinthians 2:14). And again, as he listed all the trials that come against us to overwhelm us, the great apostle said, "In all these things we are more than conquerors [super-conquerors] through him that loved us" (Romans 8:37). You should have, can have, and, bless God, will have wonderful victory when you learn to do battle from a position of truth, the way David did against Goliath.

The Bible says in 1 Samuel 17:1-3 that the armies of the Philistines and the armies of Israel stood on the sides of two mountains with a valley in between. They were preparing for battle when something unusual happened. "And there went out a champion out of the camp of the Philistines, named Goliath, of Gath, whose height was six cubits and a span" (v. 4).

We'll see later how he was dressed for battle, but notice Goliath's defiant challenge to the armies of Israel and ultimately to the God of Israel:

> And he stood and cried unto the armies of Israel, and said unto them, Why are ye come out to set your battle in array? am I not a Philistine, and ye servants to Saul? choose you a man for you, and let him come down to me. If he be able to fight with me, and to kill me, then will we be your servants: but if I prevail against him, and kill him, then shall ye be our servants, and serve us. And the Philistine said, I defy the

armies of Israel this day; give me a man, that we may fight together.

—vv. 8-10

Now when Goliath made his challenge, Saul and his army "were dismayed, and greatly afraid" (v. 11). A few verses later we are told that Goliath did this every morning and evening for forty days with no takers (v. 16).

Between these verses there is something like a parenthesis in verses 12-15 where David is introduced. He is just a youngster at this time, perhaps in his early teens. He hadn't even started to shave yet. The Bible says in verse 42 that David was "ruddy, and of a fair countenance." I take that to mean he had a little peach fuzz on his chin.

So David was a teenage boy whose three oldest brothers had gone off to battle with King Saul against the Philistines, who seemed to be the perpetual enemy of Israel. So there were the two armies drawn up against each other, and Goliath was making his challenge every day.

I imagine that like any red-blooded boy, David wished he could see that battle. We need to remember that he had already been in Saul's service as a player of the harp (see 1 Samuel 16:14-23); so he had been at the royal court.

But David had to go back home to Bethlehem and take care of the sheep until the day his daddy Jesse said to him, "Your brothers in the army need some home cooking." Jesse sent David to the army with provisions for his brothers and their commander (vv. 17-22). I suppose David jumped at the chance, wanting to get out there where the action was and maybe see a good fight.

But when David got to the front there was not a fight at all, just a shouting match—and the other side was doing most of the shouting. He looked across the valley, and there was the biggest man he had ever seen. Goliath was at least nine feet tall; some say as much as ten or eleven feet in height. He was the Incredible Hulk of his day, the original Bigfoot.

David watched and listened as Goliath came out, cursing and swearing and defying the armies of Israel. The Bible tells us that he was dressed in brass armor, and in my imagination I can see the polished brass glistening in the sunlight and can hear it clanking as this mountain of a man came walking toward Israel's army. He must have been an awesome sight.

Goliath stood there, lifting his big fist to the heavens and waving his spear with a fifteen-pound head on it, cursing and blaspheming God. The giant was saying in effect, "You cowards—you weaklings! Send somebody over here to fight me man to man, winner take all. If he defeats me, we'll lay down our arms and surrender. But if I take him, the battle is ours, and you will be our servants."

David heard this and wondered, "Why doesn't somebody go over there and put that guy to sleep?" But no one was going, not even King Saul, who was himself "a mighty man of power" and taller than any other Israelite (1 Samuel 9:1-2). On the contrary, "All the men of Israel, when they saw [Goliath], fled from him, and were sore afraid" (1 Samuel 17:24).

The problem was that they were looking at the situation from a human perspective. They were terrified by Goliath and said, "We can't go. Who could defeat *him*? Look how much bigger he is than we are." But David looked at Goliath and said, "Look how much smaller he is than God is." Saul and the soldiers of Israel said, "He's too big to hit!" But David said, "He's too big to miss!"

So David decided to go and fight Goliath, with only his sling and five smooth stones, armed in the power of Almighty God. And he won the victory, killing Goliath and cutting his head off with the giant's own sword (vv. 50-51).

You know the story, but I want to look at it again and see how it applies to you and me as we consider the power of inward truth to defeat the giants in our lives. What can we learn from this story so we can be twenty-first-century giant-killers?

DAVID CAME AGAINST A VICIOUS ENEMY

I believe that Goliath of Gath is an Old Testament picture, or a type, of Satan himself. And the battle he engaged in with David illustrates not only our struggle as believers against the devil but is also a type of Jesus' victory over Satan and the forces of hell. Let me start by showing you why I believe Goliath is a picture of Satan.

Goliath Had the Measure of Satan

First of all, I see something significant about the giant's measure. His height was six cubits, he had six pieces of armor, and the iron head of his spear weighed 600 shekels (1 Samuel 17:4-7).

The threefold repetition of the number six here is interesting because in the Bible the devil's Superman is identified by the three-fold repetition of this number: 666 (Revelation 13:18). In a sense Goliath was a picture of this coming beast whose power is the working of Satan.

Goliath Had the Might of Satan

The Bible also speaks of Goliath's might in verse 4 of our story, where he is called a "champion." He was a Superman, a mighty man, a powerful person. Again this reminds us of the power of our enemy Satan.

The Bible says, "Be sober, be vigilant; because your adversary the devil, as a roaring lion, walketh about, seeking whom he may devour" (1 Peter 5:8). Paul tells us, "We wrestle not against flesh and blood, but against principalities, against powers, against the rulers of the darkness of this world, against spiritual wickedness in high places" (Ephesians 6:12). Goliath was almost superhuman in his size and strength. He was no ordinary adversary.

Goliath Had the Manner of Satan

The Philistine giant's manner also reminds us of Satan. "And the Philistine said, I defy the armies of Israel this day" (v. 10). And when David came out to meet him, Goliath "cursed David by his gods" and told him, "I will give thy flesh unto the fowls of the air, and to the beasts of the field" (vv. 43-44).

How arrogant and defiant Goliath was. How rebellious he was against the things of God, and what fear he was causing— the same manner and defiant attitude Satan uses to try and intimidate God's people today.

Goliath roared like a lion when he saw David. I'm sure the soldiers of Israel again took off running back to their tents when they heard him. And just like Goliath, Satan is making more noise today than perhaps ever before, and saints are folding up and running away when they ought to be standing for the light and the truth of God.

A lion roars to intimidate and strike fear into his prey even when he is too far away to attack. I'm told that an adult male lion's roar can be heard up to five miles away. Now that's a lot of intimidation, considering that it's the female lion that usually does the hunting. The devil may be a roaring lion, but he's a toothless lion against God's people because he was defeated at the cross. Don't be afraid of Satan's noise, just as David wasn't afraid of Goliath's threats.

Goliath Had the Motive of Satan

I see also a reminder of Satan in Goliath's motive, which was to destroy the people and the work of God. Goliath wanted to defeat Israel's champion and make God's people slaves of the Philistines (v. 9). He also defied the armies of Israel. In other words, Goliath was against the people of God, just as the devil always has been.

According to verse 16, Goliath came out to taunt Israel twice every day for forty days. The number forty in the Bible is the number of testing and of trial. Moses was in the wilderness forty years. Israel wandered through the wilderness forty years. Jesus fasted forty days in the wilderness before being tempted by the devil (Matthew 4:2). Here is Goliath, who pictures our enemy the devil, taunting and testing God's people for forty days with the same motive as Satan—to destroy them.

DAVID ENGAGED IN A VICARIOUS ENCOUNTER

David faced a vicious enemy in Goliath and met the Philistine giant in a vicarious encounter. And in this I see a second truth we can learn for our lives today.

Vicarious means in another's place. It speaks of one standing in the place of another as a substitute. This is what David did when he went out to meet Goliath. The giant wanted one man from Israel to fight it out with him, with the fate of each army at stake. One man was to fight and win the battle in the place of all the people.

Therefore, not only do I believe that Goliath is a picture of Satan, but I believe that David is a picture of our Savior. Here we have a prefiguring of the Lord Jesus Christ, who fought for us a vicarious encounter with Satan himself. David stood for all Israel that day, just as the Lord Jesus went to bloody Calvary and stood for you and for me that day.

David prefigures and pictures the Lord Jesus so much in the Bible that Jesus was often called the "son of David" (Mark 10:47) when He was on earth. Now Jesus is certainly David's greater Son, but David is like the Savior in many ways. I want you to see just four of these similarities.

David Was the Sanctified One

Some time before David's encounter with Goliath, he had been anointed as the new king of Israel by Samuel (1 Samuel 16:13). David was just a lad at the time, but God sent the prophet Samuel to anoint him because God had rejected Saul as king because of his disobedience. When Samuel poured anointing oil on David, the Bible says, "The Spirit of the LORD came upon David from that day forward."

David was anointed with oil, symbolizing the Holy Spirit who came upon him and set him aside for God's work. He wasn't an ordinary man. He was, like our Lord, a sanctified man, although Jesus was sanctified in a greater way than even David. God said of His Son, "Therefore God, even thy God, hath anointed thee with the oil of gladness above thy fellows" (Hebrews 1:9).

David Was the Sent One

After David was sanctified by the anointing of the Holy Spirit, he was sent to face the enemy, another way in which he prefigures Christ. David's father Jesse sent him to the battlefront with bread for his brothers.

Jesus was sent to bring bread to His brethren. Jesus said to Israel, "I am that bread of life," the true bread the people were looking for (John 6:48). Jesus is pictured in 1 Samuel 17 in the bread David brought to his brothers, even if He is seen perhaps only faintly in a shadow. I believe the whole Bible somehow and in some way is about the Lord Jesus. I'd rather see Him too much in the Bible than to see Him too little.

David Was the Scorned One

David came with life-giving bread for his brethren, but what happened when he arrived? "Eliab his eldest brother heard when he spake unto the men; and Eliab's anger was kindled against David, and he said, Why camest thou down hither? and with whom has thou left those few sheep in the wilderness? I know thy pride, and the naughtiness of thine heart; for thou art come down that thou mightest see the battle" (1 Samuel 17:28).

David was treated with scorn and ridicule by his brother Eliab. And when David turned to others around him for help, they scorned and rejected him too (vv. 29-30).

David was at the battlefront on a mission from his father, but he met with rejection. The Bible says that when Jesus came on His mission from the Father in heaven, He met with similar ridicule and rejection. He was "despised and rejected of men; a man of sorrows, and acquainted with grief" (Isaiah 53:3).

Again, "He came unto his own, and his own received him not" (John 1:11).

David Was the Saving One

Praise the Lord that neither the story of David nor the story of our Lord Jesus ends with rejection. David the scorned one became David the saving one when he single-handedly won the battle that day for all of Israel. What a wonderful picture of the saving work of Jesus Christ, who, the Bible says, "died for all, that they which live should not henceforth live unto themselves, but unto him which died for them, and rose again" (2 Corinthians 5:15).

DAVID PROVIDES US WITH A VICTORIOUS EXAMPLE

Here is the third lesson I want to leave with you as we close this chapter and this book about the importance of standing for light and truth. David triumphed in his vicarious encounter against a vicious enemy, and in so doing he provides us with a victorious example.

In this David is also a type of the Lord Jesus Christ, who in the days of His flesh won the battle against our archenemy, the devil, "leaving us an example, that ye should follow his steps" (1 Peter 2:21). Jesus fought and won the battle so long ago, and yet there is a continuing battle today that we must fight.

Now make no mistake. The battle is already won, and yet in a sense it needs to be fought and won day by day. What I'm saying is that because of Calvary, we fight not *for* victory, but *from* the victory that Jesus has already secured for us.

But we must fight anyway, and because of what Jesus did on the cross, we can win our battle day by day. So as we continue

David's story, I want you to see some further blueprints for us as twenty-first-century giant-killers.

What is the giant in your life? Is it lust, envy, fear, greed, doubt? What stands between you and the joy and victory God wants you to have? There is a victorious example in 1 Samuel 17 that will help you live like a king. There are four principles we need to consider here.

The Principle of Persistence

Any battle is going to be won by those who are persistent. When David was brought to King Saul, he said, "Let no man's heart fail because of [Goliath]; thy servant will go and fight with this Philistine" (1 Samuel 17:32). David purposed in his heart he would do it, and he was not deterred by anything.

There was plenty going on around him to deter him. There was, for example, the *dismay* of others. The Bible says that Saul and the whole Israeli army "were dismayed, and greatly afraid" because of Goliath (v. 11; see also v. 24).

Fear is infectious, but David wasn't daunted. You might as well know right now that when you are in your battle, you will find around you cowardly, weak-kneed people who say it cannot be done. And if you're not careful, their fear is going to infect you. David was persistent in the face of the dismay of others. The fear of man made Saul a coward. The fear of God made David a hero. David had his eyes upon God, and therefore he was filled with purpose.

He was also persistent in spite of the *disdain* of others. We have seen how Eliab scorned David for talking so big when he was so small (v. 28). Can you hear Eliab as he curls his lip in disdain? "Hey, sonny, this is for the big boys. You don't have any right being here. Get on back there in the wilderness with those sheep."

People disdained David, and they are going to look down upon you. Did you know that the devil has laughed many believers out of victory? People sneer at us, and we fold up and run away. They laughed at David, and doubtless their laughter hurt, but he refused to let up or back up or shut up.

David also faced *discouragement* as he pursued his purpose to fight Goliath. "And Saul said to David, Thou art not able to go against this Philistine to fight with him: for thou art but a youth, and he a man of war from his youth" (v. 33).

Saul was the king of Israel, and more than that, he was an expert in warfare. Saul the expert was saying it couldn't be done. When you get ready to live for God, when you get ready to take a sling and cross that valley to face your Goliath, you're going to face these same three enemies: dismay, disdain, and discouragement.

You had better learn to close these people out and get alone with God in the secret counsel halls of the Almighty. You must get your eyes on God or you're going to lose the battle. If you start listening to those who say you haven't got what it takes, who laugh at you, or who discourage you, you are going to have a hard time facing your Goliath from a position of victory.

David had his eyes on God. The Lord was his strength, his shield, and his helper. David said, "I don't care what Saul, Eliab, or anybody else says. I want to know what God says."

It's amazing how many battles in life are won not by brilliance but by dogged persistence in carrying out God's purpose for us. It is said that half the battle is just showing up. The reason some of us aren't winning the battle is because we never show up. We don't say, "I'm going to do what the Lord told me to do, no matter who or what."

One man was bragging about what a great Christian he was. "I'm not afraid of the devil," he said. But that's not the question. Is the devil afraid of you? The Bible says, "Resist the devil, and he will flee from you" (James 4:7). That's a great promise, but it means we have to show up and stand firm.

The Principle of Progression

David illustrates another principle that is so valuable for us as we seek to live for Christ today. This is the principle of progression.

When Saul told David he couldn't face Goliath, David told him, "Thy servant kept his father's sheep, and there came a lion, and a bear, and took a lamb out of the flock: and I went after him, and smote him, and delivered it out of his mouth: and when he arose against me, I caught him by his beard, and smote him, and slew him. Thy servant slew both the lion and the bear: and this uncircumcised Philistine shall be as one of them" (1 Samuel 17:34-36).

Do you see the progression here? Before David fought Goliath, he killed a lion and a bear by the power of God. And because he had won those battles, he was ready for another. David had learned to go from victory to victory, even though his victories over the lion and the bear were won in private where no one else saw him.

Here is another illustration of the life of Jesus. Before the Savior met and defeated Satan at Calvary, He met and defeated Satan in the wilderness temptation (Matthew 4:1-11). Jesus met Satan in private in the wilderness so that he might meet him in public at Calvary.

Many of us are not winning our big battles because we are losing our little battles. The Bible says, "He that is faithful in that which is least is faithful also in much" (Luke 16:10). Some of us are not ready when the Incredible Hulk comes along because we haven't been faithful in the little things. If you want to know what a person is made of, watch how he handles the small issues of life.

My wife and I read a story in our daily devotions about a clerk in a bank who was due for a promotion. But one day he was in a cafeteria line and didn't realize the bank's president was behind him. The clerk picked up a pat of butter that cost a few cents and slid it under his piece of bread so he wouldn't have to pay for it at the checkout line.

But the bank president was watching and saw what the man did. The president thought, *If this man cannot be trusted with something like this, I cannot give him that promotion I wanted to give him.* The clerk lost his promotion because he was dishonest for a little bit of butter, which is about as little as you can get. But because the man was not faithful in that which was least, no one was going to give him much.

I wonder how many times God has had to pass us by for the same kind of reason. God could use David to defeat Goliath and rescue Israel because he was a faithful shepherd who determined that even though it was just one little sheep, he was going to take care of what his father had entrusted to him. And it didn't matter if anyone knew or saw what happened, because it mattered to David.

The Principle of Power

Please note that David did not go out against Goliath without any power. He had tremendous power, but it wasn't in his armament or weapons.

Not that Saul didn't try to arm David. Read 1 Samuel 17:38-39, and you'll remember that Saul gave David his armor. It must have been almost a humorous sight to see this teenager staggering around in what looked like his daddy's armor. But there would have been nothing funny about the result if David had tried to fight in the monarch's king-sized armor.

"I cannot go with these; for I have not proved them," David told Saul (v. 39). Then he took his sling, picked out five smooth stones, and moved out to meet Goliath.

In this meeting we learn the secret of David's power. The Philistine giant scorned and derided little David and threatened to break him into pieces and feed him to the pigeons (vv. 42-44).

But don't miss what David said in reply: "Thou comest to me with a sword, and with a spear, and with a shield: but I come to thee in the name of the LORD of hosts, the God of the armies of Israel, whom thou has defied. This day will the LORD deliver thee into mine hand; and I will smite thee, and take thy head from thee; and I will give the carcasses of the host of the Philistines this day unto the fowls of the air, and to the wild beasts of the earth; that all the earth may know that there is a God in Israel" (vv. 45-46).

In these verses the principle of power is delineated. What was the power that rested upon David? What enabled a teenage boy to do what he did? First of all, he had *powerful methods*. He refused King Saul's armor.

Saul was a huge man, but David was a boy trying to move around with all of this heavy armor. David wasn't even fully grown yet. Everything was lopsided on him. I had to play football one time with a helmet that was a couple of sizes too big. That was tough. Here was little David saying, "Take it off! I can't use it." Then he went back to his proven methods.

This tells us that when we fight Satan we cannot use unsanctified armor. The Bible tell us, "The weapons of our warfare are not carnal, but mighty through God to the pulling down of strongholds" (2 Corinthians 10:4). You are not going to overcome Satan with the power of positive thinking, your money, or any other technique. You cannot out-organize or out-publicize him. Our weapons are invisible and invincible.

One of the saddest things I see today is churches that are wearing the armor of Madison Avenue, trying to outdo the devil with marketing and glitz and advertising muscle. But the world can "out-world" us every time. Had David put on Saul's armor, he would have been ignominiously defeated. The weapons of our warfare are not carnal or of this world. We are told, "Put on the whole armour of God, that ye may be able to stand against the wiles of the devil" (Ephesians 6:11).

The Principle of Praise

Besides his powerful methods, David had a *powerful master*. It blesses me every time I read that David said to the giant, "I come to thee in the name of the LORD of hosts, the God of the armies of Israel." David came in the power of a name.

As Christians we come against Satan in the power of the name of Jesus. The devil does not flinch at your name or mine. But he cannot stand against the name of Jesus. Jesus said, "If ye shall ask any thing in my name, I will do it" (John 14:14).

We can come against any giant in our lives if we will come not in our name and strength but say, "Satan, I come against you in the name of Jesus."

If there is anything I have learned in my ministry, it's the power of the name of Jesus. There are times when I don't even know what to pray. So I just bow my head and repeat, "Jesus is Lord" over and over. David came against Goliath in the name of the Lord of hosts, who is Jesus Christ Himself.

David also had a *powerful motive*. David revealed his motive when he told Goliath why he was going to kill him and rout the Philistines: "that all the earth may know that there is a God in Israel" (v. 46).

David's motive was not to promote himself or make his name great. David's motive was the glory of God, and that's why he won the battle. Sometimes we want to win the battle, but our motive is wrong.

We have a financial problem, for instance. But we really don't want to defeat it for the glory of God, so that He might be Lord of our pocketbooks. We just want more money in the bank. We may have a relationship problem, but we don't want to get the victory over it for God's glory. We just want to be happy and not have our comfortable life disturbed.

Dear reader, when we get serious about wanting God to be glorified in us more than we want our own prosperity or happiness or comfort, then we are going to see some giants fall before us. We are going to see Satan routed before us. When we get the right method, the right master, and the right motive, we've got power. There is power in a sanctified, Spirit-filled person who says, "It doesn't matter whether I live or die, so long as God is glorified."

It is obvious that young David was not on an ego trip. He was not striving for personal profit or praise. His motive was the glory of God.

And how does God get glory to His name? Here is a formula that He often uses. He takes what the world would call an insignificant and ordinary person and with that person does extraordinary things. The result is glory to God Himself. Remember that David was a shepherd boy who gained victory over a massive giant. There was no other explanation except that God had given a supernatural victory, and therefore all praise was due to Him. Paul taught the same principle in the New Testament:

> For ye see your calling, brethren, how that not many wise men after the flesh, not many mighty, not many noble, are called: But God hath chosen the foolish things of the world to confound the wise; and God hath chosen the weak things of the world to confound the things which are mighty; And base things of the world, and things which are despised, hath God chosen, yea, and things which are not, to bring to nought things that are: That no flesh should glory in his presence. But of him are ye in Christ Jesus, who of God is made unto us wisdom, and righteousness, and sanctification, and redemption: That, according as it is written, He that glorieth, let him glory in the Lord.
>
> —1 CORINTHIANS 1:26-31

Throughout his life David refused personal glory for this event. He never signed his name, King David, G.G.K. (Great Giant-Killer). When we begin to take the glory, God will stop giving the victory.

Years ago in Florida where I was pastoring, we decided to do something to reach young people. So we had what we called a "Week of Champions." We invited stellar athletes from across the country to come to a gymnasium and give Christian testimonies.

It was a wonderful event. One of those who gave a testimony was Paul Anderson, who was at that time carrying the title of the strongest man in the world. Paul had enormous strength. He lifted more weight on his back than any living man had ever done. His testimony was electrifying. In essence he said, "If the strongest man in the world needs Jesus, so do you."

The next Sunday in our church a college student came forward to profess his new faith in Christ. I asked him when he had come to know the Lord Jesus. He said, "During the Week of Champions."

I asked, "What night?"

"The night Paul Anderson was there."

I said, "Wasn't Paul Anderson's testimony incredible?"

"I don't remember Paul Anderson's testimony," he replied. When I asked him what it was that convicted him, he said, "It was the testimony of_____," and he mentioned a name of a person that I had never heard of and cannot remember to this day.

"Which athlete was he?" I asked this young man.

"Oh, he was not an athlete. He was paralyzed and in a wheelchair. There was a time of free testimony, and they lifted him to the platform. He wheeled that chair around and with a face beaming like the noonday sun told what Jesus Christ meant to him."

That college student said to me, "Sir, when I saw the victory that man had in spite of his physical disability, I knew that his faith was real, and I knew that I needed to be saved."

I have thought about that often. In that gym that night was the strongest man in the world, and yet God used an unheralded man in a wheelchair to bring a student to Christ.

Indeed, God has "chosen the weak things of the world to confound the things which are mighty." And in doing so He gets glory to Himself. That is the principle of praise.

May God give you that holy resolve as you commit yourself to stand for the light of God and the truth of God. God be with you!